Ciara Mulcahy

Science
Displays

GEORGIE BEASLEY AND
ANN MOBERLEY

AUTHORS GEORGIE BEASLEY AND ANN MOBERLEY

EDITOR SUSAN HOWARD

ASSISTANT EDITOR LESLEY SUDLOW

SERIES DESIGNER LYNNE JOESBURY

DESIGNER SARAH ROCK

ILLUSTRATIONS CATHY HUGHES

PHOTOGRAPHS MARTYN CHILLMAID

With thanks to Miss Andrea Conroy, Nursery NNEB, who helped with all the displays and to all the parents and children at Moons Moat First School, Redditch.

Designed using Adobe Pagemaker

Published by Scholastic Ltd, Villiers House, Clarendon Avenue, Leamington Spa, Warwickshire CV32 5PR
Text © Georgie Beasley and Ann Moberley

© 2000 Scholastic Ltd

6 7 8 9 0   5 6

British Library Cataloguing-in-Publication Data
A catalogue record for this book is available from the British Library.

ISBN 0-439-01637-1

SCIENCE

Contents

Introduction

The importance of display

Displays are a vital part of all early years settings, providing an opportunity for interactive, cross-curricular learning incorporating the children's own work. *Themes on Display Science* aims to provide advice and support to enable all early years educators to teach the scientific element of the Knowledge and Understanding of the World area of learning through display.

The ideas in this book can be used as starting points for the organization of structured play activities through which very young children learn best and which provide for progression in learning about the world around them. Each display is a mixture of interactive activity and a celebration of children's work, which motivates and encourages

additional learning. Some can be used as instant displays to spark initial interest for a new topic. Each set of displays is planned to be produced over a half-term and is organized so that all children, including those who attend part-time, can be fully involved in its production.

Themes on Display Science contains five chapters based on popular early years themes.

In Chapter 1, Animals, children have the opportunity to learn about a range of creatures, both familiar and unfamiliar. There's a vibrant display based on animals and birds of the rainforest and children are encouraged to think about caring for animals with a display about pets.

Chapter 2 looks at Growing, and provides opportunities for children to think not only about how people grow from babies to adults, but also about

Introduction

growth of plants and animals around them. The favourite story of 'Jack and the Beanstalk' is the stimulus for an exciting two-part display which includes a giant beanstalk that 'grows' up and across the ceiling.

Chapter 3 focuses on Water, beginning with a stunning waterfall stimulus display. Children are encouraged to think about the many ways in which we use water, and about the creatures that live in water.

Chapter 4 explores Materials. Children are asked to explore and investigate a wide variety of different materials, learning about their properties and their uses. There are opportunities to make a 'feely' texture display, to explore shiny materials and to sort items into sets depending on whether they are magnetic or non-magnetic.

The final chapter, Minibeasts, provides opportunities for children to find out about the lives and habitats of a variety of tiny creatures from spiders in their webs to worms under the ground.

Each chapter begins with a stimulus display to introduce the theme and stimulate the children's interest. You may like to ask parents and carers for contributions from home to add to the display and for their help in setting it up and supporting the children. Following the stimulus display there are five interactive displays. These extend the theme of the chapter, encouraging the children to explore the topic and to ask questions to extend their knowledge. Each chapter concludes with a tabletop display, which provides opportunities for children to have hands-on experience of resources relating to the topic and to sort items. There are also ideas for further display tables to extend the theme.

Full-colour photographs throughout the book show the detail of each display, illustrating how the techniques, materials and colours have been chosen to create the best effect. The text gives clear guidance on how to plan the displays and includes easy-to-follow instructions to enable anyone who works in an early years setting to reproduce them effectively.

Using the book

Each display is broken down into various sub-headings:

● Learning objective

A specific learning objective linked to the scientific element of the Knowledge and understanding of the world area of learning is given at the beginning of each display. It states clearly what the children are expected to have learned at the completion of the display.

Particular attention is given to developing the children's respect for all living things and an awareness of environmental issues.

● **What you need**

A detailed list provides information on all the resources required to complete the display. The resources should be readily available in most early years settings, or they may need to be brought in by the children or collected from the local area. The list is designed to be flexible, and you can substitute resources as appropriate.

Specific guidance is given on colour schemes and the different materials required. Details of the sizes and types of papers, fabrics and recycled materials, the range of colouring medium and any items, objects and collections used are included. Objects required for creating specific effects are detailed and there is clear information on how to create effective labels, borders and titles. Guidance on the most effective ways of fixing the elements of the display to the background is also provided.

● **What to do**

This section gives a step-by-step guide to creating the display. Clear information is given on the type of wall and/or table-top space required, or how to make use of awkwardly-shaped areas. There is advice about the most effective colours to use for the display, including ideas for background colours and coverings for any boxes used.

The techniques used to create the different effects are explained in detail, and advice is given on why each material is chosen. There is also advice on organizing the activities, resources, children and additional adults. Borders are an important part of the display, and there are ideas for creating effective borders to direct the observer's eye to the key parts of the display. Labelling and different types of titles are also covered.

● **Talk about**

This section includes ideas on what to talk about during and after the production of the display. Ideas on the development of language and the early scientific skills associated with observation and sorting, particularly noticing similarities and differences, are given. Health and safety issues are covered and there are suggestions for questions to challenge and extend children's thinking.

Introduction

THEMES ON DISPLAY for early years

● **Home links**
Parents and carers play a vital part in their children's development, and this section provides many suggestions for creating and maintaining those links with home. These include ideas on how carers and parents can come into the setting to help the children make the different elements of the displays and how they can contribute unusual items from home. There are also suggestions for ways in which parents can extend the theme and reinforce the learning objective with their child while they are out and about.

It is strongly suggested that you follow your own setting's policy when inviting visitors in to talk and work with the children.

● **Curriculum links**
At the end of each display, suggestions are given on ways to use the display to contribute to the development of the six areas of learning. This section provides follow-up opportunities for extension and support to Personal, social and emotional development, including religious education; Language and literacy, including the development of role-play; Mathematics, with particular reference to numeracy; other elements of Knowledge and understanding of the world, including ICT, geography, history and D&T; Physical development, both fine and gross motor skills; and Creative development including music, art and dance.

Many ideas can be repeated in a number of the displays. For example, the development of the children's early literacy skills to listen for, hear and identify rhymes is suggested in the display entitled 'Spiders' on page 64. Although it has not also been suggested in other displays, this idea can be extended in all those which lend themselves to the use of rhymes.

Making the displays interactive
Children get the most from the displays when they are able to interact with them through structured play activities. The 'Material textures' display on page 60 develops children's natural curiosity for exploration and investigation. Mathematical skills of counting and sequencing are developed effectively through the 'Water all around us' display on page 38, when the children are invited to count the items of washing on the line. The 'Sealife' display on page 46 encourages children to make their own fish, which develops creative ability and the fine motor skills of drawing and colouring through a fun, play activity.

For many of the display ideas, children are encouraged to work individually and in groups to add things to the display themselves. One example of this is the 'Pets' display on page 18, which involves the children making handprints to create a picture of a guinea pig. They also paint pictures of their own pets and bring in photographs from home to add to the table-top display in the 'Animals' chapter. Encourage children to interact with displays by making them as inviting as possible.

Choose your materials carefully: use Velcro to attach elements so that children can remove and replace them, slotting them into the correct place. Add moveable labels and challenge children to replace them in the correct places. Add games to a display table which stimulate children to refer to the display and include small-world toys for them to create their own scenes in front of the display. Let the children add their own items from home, such as favourite toys or pictures.

Planning displays
It is very important that display is included in the planning process and involves all staff. The environment of the setting plays a vital role in providing a stimulating, motivating and interesting

learning environment and can only be effective to learning if all staff who work in the setting develop its planned use. Display will only be used effectively to support children's learning if the opportunities for structured play activities are identified beforehand. In the 'Water all around us' display on page 38 for example, the sorting pegs activity is set within a progressively planned programme to develop early sorting skills.

Guidance is given on how to collect items, organize parents and carers to contribute and how to produce the stimulus displays to orchestrate the response you want.

Stimulus displays
The stimulus displays outlined in this book can be put up relatively quickly and then stored away for future use. It is a good idea to build up a bank of such displays, which can be used to spark the children's interest and enthusiasm for a new topic.

In addition to the display items in your pack, include templates; examples of photocopiable sheets used; labels and lettering for the title and a variety of drapes.

Also include a copy of your letter to parents to send at the beginning of a new topic asking for their support and giving them information on what the children will learn during the half-term.

Display tables
Select tables with shapes which complement the display and which are easily accessible. Choose a table which is the correct height and depth for the space available and which will show off the items in your collection to best effect. Collect various drapes and fabrics in a range of colours and a variety of textures to cover the tables. Different-sized cardboard boxes can be used to create a variety of heights for the display and will add interest to the items in your collection. Arrange the cardboard boxes on the table before you cover them with the drape, or cover them with paper of a complementary or contrasting colour before arranging them on a covered table.

Constructing aesthetic displays
Choose your colours carefully and plan to use more than one texture in your display. The use of unusual materials to create different textures is effective if the texture matches the purpose and required effect. For example, in the 'Birds' display on page 22, an old patterned towel has been sculptured to make the trunk of a tree to good effect,

SCIENCE

while in the 'Pondlife' display on page 44, bubble wrap has been used to create frogspawn.

Children need to be encouraged to think about what the display is showing them, to raise questions, to talk about the various elements, and to feel a sense of achievement that their own work is on show. You can achieve this in various ways:

● add appropriate information and story books

● invite the children to contribute articles from home, favourite toys or mementoes from visits

● take photographs of the children working to foster enthusiasm as a display develops and to provide a record of achievement

● use unusual and interesting materials such as feathers, reclaimed materials, sequins and natural materials

● use a range of colouring materials from pastels to bright poster paints.

Creating 2-D and 3-D displays

There are many techniques you can employ to make displays two- and three-dimensional. In the 'Worms' display on page 68, old tights or stockings are stuffed with dried beans or small, scrunched-up newspaper balls before being painted. In the 'Rain and shine' display on page 42, card and a sponge have been fixed to the display board behind the open umbrella so that the top opens outwards, over the head of the child in the picture, and away from the display. In both the 'Pondlife' display on page 44 and 'Worms' on page 68, frames constructed of chicken wire are covered with papier mâché to create three-dimensional models, before being painted.

You can create interest and add depth by suspending elements at different heights and distances fom your display board. Experiment with different techniques to find the best effect.

Using awkward areas

In this book, there are several examples where awkward areas have been successfully utilized into the display. In the 'I can see through' display on page 52 of the Materials chapter, for example, windows play an important part in the overall composition of the display. The 'Ladybirds, caterpillars and butterflies' display on page 62 illustrates how a small strip of wall and a door have been used to depict a hedgerow which curls its way along and around awkward obstacles. For the 'Jack and the beanstalk' display on page 30, the long, winding beanstalk travels up the wall and across the ceiling space to connect several interacting displays.

Mounting and framing

It is important to show children that their contributions are valued and this can be achieved through careful mounting and backing of individual pieces of work. Thoughtful use of colour, shape and texture and the imaginative arrangement of work on the display board help to create additional interest, which creates a stimulating environment and motivates children to interact with the display.

Mount the children's pictures on paper of a contrasting colour to provide a frame which draws attention to the picture and shows it off to best effect. Use a glue stick to apply adhesive to the outside edges and centre of the picture before sticking to a piece of paper which will give a border of approximately one centimetre all the way around.

Make titles stand out by double-mounting lettering to create a border or shadow. Black is an effective colour, or you may prefer to use a colour which contrasts with the main colour of the letters. For example the title for the 'Ladybirds, caterpillars and butterflies' display on page 62 is an example of how black and red have been used to give the title a three-dimensional shape with a dropped-shadow effect, making it stand out from the display. The choice of colour was deliberate to complement the colours of the ladybirds.

Free-standing labels made from card are particularly effective as they can be moved around the display by the children. The 'Material textures' table-top display on page 60 is a good example of how this idea has been used to make the display truly interactive.

Borders

The effective use of borders around a display helps to lead the eye to the different components. It is important that you take as much time to plan your border as you do the main elements of the display. Make use of children's work such as patterns or prints, or stick to contrasting or complementary strips of colour. Introduce interesting effects, such as rippling the paper by stapling it at intervals, or try using paper with scalloped edges.

Labels and titles

Clear, bold labelling is an important part of any display. Try to use a variety of techniques and a range of materials and textures to add interest. In 'Bubbles' on page 40, the title is spelled out using bubble writing. The title for the 'Worms' display on page 68 is made by cutting worm-shaped letters from brown paper.

Draw around letter stencils to create clean lines, or let the shape of the letters reflect the content of the display. Let the

children use the word-processor to create short captions, and make use of the children's own labels to add to their individual drawings and paintings. Use labels that can be removed and reattached in different places.

Cutting and fixing

A guillotine is essential to make a clean edge when cutting paper and gives clear measurement support. Use scissors only when a straight cut is not required or if you are making a border with a fancy line. Attach the items to the display with staples or glue so that the fixing is almost invisible and does not detract from the attractiveness of the display. Drawing pins should only be used when initially setting out the display, in the planning stages. If you are using moveable labels, fix them to the board using Velcro or write them on to folded pieces of thick card.

Useful resources

Many of the resources suggested are readily available in most early years settings, but there are a few specialist resource items that are useful to have:
● a sturdy gun stapler and staples to fit
● a small stapler and staples to fit
● sticky tape
● display pins
● guillotine strimmer
● glue sticks
● rolls of good quality, non-fade, backing paper in a variety of colours, which can also be used to create interesting borders

● supplies of tissue, crêpe and Cellophane papers to add texture
● a selection of textiles in a range of interesting patterns and bright colours including tablecloths, towels and old curtains
● good quality PVA glue and spreaders
● a range of paintbrushes and powder-paint colours
● a range of papers, fabrics and wool off-cuts sorted into colours and stored in suitable containers
● interesting collage materials with different textures and colours, such as feathers and fake fur fabric
● good quality scissors for adult use
● collections of magazines, comics, mail order catalogues and holiday brochures
● a range of cardboard boxes and other interesting shaped containers in a variety of different shapes and sizes.

Useful contacts

Many high street firms support early years settings and are only too pleased to contribute to displays. Useful sources include printing companies, who are often willing to supply unwanted offcuts of paper and card free of charge if you are willing to collect.

Shops are usually pleased to donate display items with which they have recently finished and are good sources of collage materials and free-standing display boards. You will probably find that office stationers often have display Christmas cards and out-of-date calendars and diaries which they may be willing to donate.

Animals

Animals of the world

Learning objective: to learn about the animals around us.

What you need
Animal gift wrap; green sugar paper; animal sponge prints; magazines with pictures of animals; paint; animal templates; gummed paper; animal posters, postcards and pictures; fiction and non-fiction books; soft toys; animal ornaments; stapler; plain fabric; labels.

What to do
Cover a small display board with animal gift wrap. Ask the children to draw around animal templates onto gummed paper and to carefully cut them out. Alternatively, invite them to make sponge prints or to cut pictures from magazines. Make sure that they cut or print only one type of animal from each colour, so for example, all the rabbits might be yellow. Stick the shapes in a repeating pattern onto the strips of green paper to make a border.

Display posters, postcards and pictures of animals on your board. Include posters of baby animals to help develop the children's language skills. Place a table in front of the display and cover it with fabric. Arrange your collection of animal toys and ornaments, and fiction and non-fiction books at different levels and spaced out. If you wish, you could label your animal objects with either hand-written or word-processed labels.

In this chapter you will find ideas for creating a range of stunning displays about all sorts of animals, from sheep and cows on the farm to colourful parrots and crocodiles in the rainforest

Talk about
● Look at the animals around the border. What do the children notice about the pattern?
● Talk about the animals on display. Are they wild animals or pets? Can the children tell you where any of them live?
● Introduce the names of the baby animals, for example, pig, piglet; sheep, lamb and so on. Invite the children to add any that they may know.

Home links
● Invite parents and carers to contribute non-valuable animal ornaments, animal toys and other animal items such as children's animal slippers!
● Develop an animal book lending library for parents and carers to share with their child at home.

SCIENCE

Noah's ark

Learning objective: to learn that there are all kinds of animals in the world.

What you need

A display board and surface; blue backing paper; various colours of paint; paper; card; black sugar paper; labels; paintbrushes; pale blue card; gold paper; silver foil; blue and green Cellophane; scraps of blue papers and fabrics, including tissue, sugar and crêpe; glue; stapler; scissors; pinking shears; light blue cotton and a sewing needle; letter templates or pre-cut letters; scalloped blue card; a collection of model wild, domesticated and farm animals.

What to do

Tell the children the story of Noah and the flood. If possible, show them an illustrated story and ask them to name and count the animals. Tell the children that they are going to make a colourful display is going to include pictures of some of the animals that were on board the ark.

Cover the display board with blue backing paper. Cut the shape of the hull and cabin of an ark from gold paper. Invite a small group of children to paint a trapezium of red paper for the roof. When dry, staple the cabin and roof in the centre of the display board. Leaving the top edge open, staple the hull onto the display board, letting the paper sit away from the wall to create a three-dimensional effect.

Invite the children to decide which animals they would like to include in the display – giraffes, elephants, tigers and zebras create a dramatic and interesting picture. Let the children work together to paint pairs of animal heads. When dry, cut the animals out and staple them inside the ark. Ask the children to paint other pairs of animals such as fish, butterflies or birds to add around the ark.

Use pinking shears to cut out large oval shapes from light blue card to make raindrops. Ask the children to cover one side of the raindrop with silver foil and the other with a collage of blue papers. An adult should use a sewing needle to attach the cotton to the top of each raindrop. Suspend the raindrops in front of the display.

Beneath the ark, staple strips of blue and green

Cellophane to create waves. Complete the board by stapling a white dove cut from card above the ark. Cut the letters to spell the learning objective from black sugar paper and add these to the display to make a title. Attach a border made from scalloped blue card and add the names of the animals on labels onto the hull of the ark.

If you have space, add a table in front of your display and invite the children to place the animal models along the table, so that they look as if they are boarding the ark.

Talk about
● Look at the different animals on board the ark. Which animals have spots? Which have stripes? Invite the children to describe the different patterns and colours that they can see.
● Talk about keeping safe around animals. Why do some animals bite or scratch?
● Talk about the natural habitats of the animals in the display.
● Ask the children to think of other types of animals that they could include in the display such as insects or birds.

Home links
● Ask carers to talk to the children about animals. Which animals are safe to touch? Are any animals safe to touch without an adult present?
● Send a letter home asking whether carers have any models of unusual animals to contribute to the display. You may wish to include some examples to give them an idea of what you want.

Using the display
Personal and social development
● Read the story of *Noah's Ark* such as the version retold by Lucy Cousins (Walker). Talk about families.
● Ask the children to help you make a set of rules to promote good behaviour in your setting. Write these onto a large sheet of paper and invite the children to decorate it together.

Language and literacy
● Talk about the names of the animals in the ark. Invite the children to read the labels on the display.
● Ask the children to retell the story using toy animals as props.
● Read a range of animal stories, rhymes and poems.

Mathematics
● Invite the children to count the pairs of animals on the ark. How many pairs of animals make four/six/eight? What other things come in pairs? Make a collection of pairs of items.
● Make large pictures of tall, short, large, small, animals and display these by an outline of a child. Which animals are taller, shorter than the children?
● Sort models of animals into sets of, for example, those with stripes/without stripes; with spots/without spots and so on.

Knowledge and understanding of the world
● Take the children outside on a sunny day and make 'raindrops' using a hosepipe. Can the children see a rainbow?
● Give the children a copy of the photocopiable sheet on page 73. Invite them to draw lines to match the pairs of animals.

Creative development
● Invite the children to make models of other animal pairs from Plasticine or clay. Add these to the table in front of the display.

The rainforest

Learning objective: to learn about some of the animals that live in the rainforest.

What you need
A display wall; green backing paper; pale blue sheet; paint in various colours; paintbrushes; PVA glue; green crêpe paper; egg boxes; plain paper cake cases; hessian wallpaper; socks and tights; sponge pieces; white paper; red, orange and yellow poster paper; stapler; yellow fabric; red, yellow and blue tissue paper.

What to do
Before beginning the display have a discussion with the children about rainforests. Has anyone watched any television programmes about rainforests and the animals that live in them? You may have an adult in your setting who has visited a rainforest. Talk about the animals and plants and how they are different to those in this country. Discuss the importance of conserving the rainforests and the animals in them. Now invite the children to help you make a rainforest display.

Cover a wall with green backing paper. Cut green crêpe paper into strips and suspend these in loops from the ceiling in front of the display to represent vines. Sponge print the hessian wallpaper using thin brown paint then cut it into the shape of a tree trunk and branches. Staple these to the backing paper. Encourage the children to use collage, paint and sponge printing to make large leaves for the tree. Ask the children to paint, collage or sponge print strips of green paper to make ground plants.

Invite the children to make huge bright red and orange coloured flowers. Provide paper flower shapes and let them collage the shapes using squares of poster paper. Give each flower a yellow circular centre. Paint the cake cases yellow, and when dry attach these to the centre of the flowers. Cover the flowers with PVA glue to give them a shiny effect before attaching them across the bottom of the display among the green leaves.

Draw outlines of monkeys and ask the children to paint them

using thick brown paint. When dry, add the detail of arms, feet and head in a darker brown. Stick on circles of white paper for the eyes, and add a black thumb print in the centre of each one. Paint a mouth and nostrils using a pinker brown.

On either side of the display, make two sponge-printed ponds. Splatter paint a pale blue sheet using blue, black and white paint before stapling it beneath the sponge painted water to create a three-dimensional effect.

In groups, allow the children to cut out and glue egg boxes to cut-out figures of crocodiles. Paint the egg boxes in two shades of green. Stick on white paper cake cases for eyes and triangles of white paper for teeth. Use PVA to glue the crocodiles in the ponds.

Invite the children to stuff tights and socks with crumpled-up paper. Turn these into snakes by dabbing on paint and gluing squares of paper along the body. When dry, suspend them among the leaves and crêpe paper vines.

Provide the children with outlines of parrots and feather shapes cut from bright red, blue and yellow tissue paper. Mark three sections on the parrot shapes: tail and breast to be coloured blue, wing tip to be coloured yellow, and head and shoulder to be coloured red. Help the children to glue the feather shapes to the parrots in layers starting from the bottom of the tail and working their way to the top of the head. Finally, add the beak and eye using yellow tissue paper.

Cut out the letters of the learning objective from orange poster paper and display this in a prominent place.

Talk about
● Discuss the animals that live in rainforests. Explain that different animals live in different habitats in different parts of the world, for example not all snakes live in rainforests, some live in deserts; there are no monkeys in the rainforests in Australia.
● Do all the animals in the display have legs? Which ones live in trees/in the water/on the ground?

Home links
● Find out whether any parents or carers have ever been to a rainforest. Ask them if they would be willing to come in and talk to the children, showing photographs or video films if they have them.
● Ask whether parents or carers have any items with animal designs, such as wrapping paper, serviettes, silk scarves and so on, which they could lend for the display to provide additional opportunities to talk.
● Ask one or two additional adults to support the children when making the parrots. Encourage them to talk about the shape and colour of the feathers. Compare the colours of the parrots with the colour of the birds found in our country. How are they different?

Using the display
Personal, social and emotional development
● Talk about the need to care for the world's rainforests. The children are too young to understand all the issues but they can be made aware of the need to care for our environment.

Language and literacy
● Introduce the names of the animals. Many children will be unfamiliar some of the names.
● Read animal stories and rhymes such as *The Tiger who Came to Tea* by Judith Kerr (Collins).

Mathematics
● Sort the animals into sets such as legs/no legs; climb/can't climb.

Creative development
● Sing songs about the animals in the display, such as 'Never smile at a crocodile' from *Birds and Beasts* (A & C Black).
● Encourage the children to use blue and yellow paint to mix their own shades of green. Let them use the new shade to paint more leaves for the display using a variety of techniques.

SCIENCE

Pets

Learning objective: to learn that some animals live with humans.

What you need
Purple backing paper; stapler; brown, green and black paint; brown, buff and yellow coloured paper; black, orange, brown and pink wool; pipe-cleaners; black pom-poms; black buttons; PVA glue; black and white paper.

What to do
Begin by talking about pets. Who has a pet? Does anyone have any unusual pets? Tell the children that they are going to help you make a display showing some of the animals that people keep as pets.

Cover a display board with purple backing paper. Add the learning objective made from yellow letters.

Gather the children together to mass produce brown, green and black hand prints. To make the striped guinea pig, give the children sheets of white and buff paper and ask them to draw around their hands. When the prints are

dry, help the children to cut them out. Staple or glue the green hands across the centre of the board for the grass. Create the guinea pigs by stapling or gluing the hands to the board starting from the bottoms! Make eyes from circles of white paper with smaller black circles in the middle. Cut feet and ears from black and white paper.

Make a brown hand print tree trunk on the right-hand side of the board. Continue across the top of the board or along the ceiling to create branches.

Invite the children to make pets to add to the display. Let them glue wool to cat templates, then add buttons for eyes and noses, and pipe-cleaners or wool for whiskers.

Make dogs in a similar way, gluing on synthetic fur. To make a Dalmatian dog, provide templates cut from white paper and let the children finger-print black spots. Give the dogs a three-dimensional effect by adding small black pom-poms.

Attach the cats and dogs to the board interspersed with green hand prints grouped together to depict tufts of grass. Add appropriate labels of the

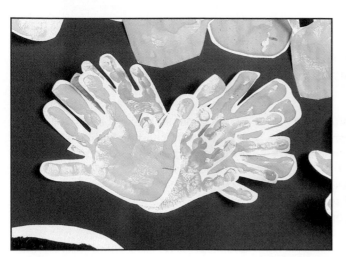

animals' names double-mounted on purple and yellow paper.

Talk about

● Invite the children to talk about their own pets at home. How do they care for their pets? What kind of food do they eat? Where do they live?

● Talk about animals that do not live with humans. Why do the children think that elephants or tigers are not kept as pets?

Home links

It is always exciting for children to see pets at first hand so, if your setting's policy allows it, let the children bring in their pets from home. It will be necessary to check that the animals have had all the appropriate injections and so on before letting the children see them, and it is not recommended that the animals are handled by the children. Always check for allergies beforehand and inform parents and carers.

● Ask parents and carers to bring in photographs of the children's pets and any accessories that they can spare to add to the display.

● Ask adults to come into the setting to help with the production of hand prints.

Using the display
Personal, social and emotional development

● Set up the hands production activity so that the children work together as a team. They can also be encouraged to work together to produce the cats, dogs and other pets.

Language and literacy

● Read stories, rhymes and poems about pets such as *When Martha's Away* by Bruce Ingman (Mammoth) or *The Three Little Guinea Pigs* by Peter Kavanagh (Little Hippo).

● Ask the children to draw pictures of their pets. Write the pets' names and add a simple sentence. If the children are unable to write themselves, model the writing for them.

Mathematics

● Sort the wool into sets of colours.

● Talk about the shape of the pom-poms. Are they round? Do they have points or corners?

● Do a survey among the children to find out about the different pets. Make a block graph of the results. Which is the most popular pet?

Knowledge and understanding of the world

● Develop descriptive language by comparing two different animals, such as a cat and dog or a fish and budgerigar. Make a list of the similarities and differences that the children suggest.

Physical development

● Develop the movement of animals in a gymnastics lesson. Good animals to use are rabbit, fish, horse, dog and cat. Discuss the animals which move in a similar way and those whose movements are very different.

● Draw a simple goldfish outline. Provide photocopies for the children to create their own fish handwriting patterns.

● Invite the children to make their own pom-poms by winding wool around a circle of card.

Creative development

● Allow the children to do free paintings of their pets. When dry, cut these out and mount them onto a complementary colour before displaying them alongside the collection of pet accessories.

The farm

Learning objective: to learn about some of the animals which live on a farm.

What you need
Blue backing paper; pink, different-coloured tissue paper; two shades of green crêpe paper; hay; washed sheep's wool; pink paint; white, gold, black, yellow and blue paper; PVA glue; stapler; yellow card border; scissors; buttons; feathers; red and yellow felt.

What to do
Explain to the children that they are going to make a farmyard display to learn about some of the different animals which live on a farm.

Cover the display board with blue backing paper. Create rolling fields by stapling shades of green tissue and crêpe paper in sections over the middle third of the board. At the bottom of the board, staple yellow tissue and gold and yellow paper to make the farmyard floor. Ask the children to glue hay to the bottom right-hand corner of the board. Add two white clouds cut from white paper, peeping over the green fields. Finally, staple the yellow border around the display, rippling it to add interest. Make the animals as follows:
● Sheep: Cover two white 'clouds' (one large and one small for each sheep) with washed sheep's wool. Back them with black paper and staple them to the board to make the body and tail of the

sheep. Make faces with black paper cut in a triangular shape with curved corners. Add buttons for eyes and triangles for ears. Finally, add four rectangles of black paper for the legs.
● Pigs: Use the children's own paintings of pink pigs. When dry, cut them out and

glue scrunched-up pink tissue paper to the body. Add black tissue paper eyes.

Mount the pigs on black paper before stapling them to the display.
● Chicks: Invite the children to draw and paint their own chicks before gluing on scrunched-up tissue paper. Mount on black paper before stapling to the bottom left of the board.

Make two hens by gluing real feathers or tissue-paper shapes to the children's drawings. Make the crown with red felt and the beak with yellow. Mount onto black paper and staple to the board above the chicks. Staple painted black and white cows to the right of the picture, above the hay.

Finally, invite a child to paint the sun and finish the display by adding the learning objective as a title using yellow letters.

Using the display
Personal, social and emotional development
● Read the story of 'The Little Red Hen' (traditional) and talk about sharing with the children.

Language and literacy
● Make large pictures of the story of 'The Little Red Hen' and sequence the story together in a large wall display. Invite the children to use the pictures to retell the story in their own words.

Mathematics
● Count the number of pigs, hens, cows and so on in your picture.
● Sort the animals by colour, number of legs and so on.

Knowledge and understanding of the world
● Make some bread together. Talk about the change that happens during the cooking process.

Creative development
● Make up a short story about a farm and invite the children to pretend to be different animals, moving appropriately and making farmyard noises!
● Sing 'Old MacDonald Had a Farm', encouraging the children to join in with the animal noises.

Talk about
● Discuss the animals in the display. Can the children think of any other animals which live on a farm?
● Challenge the children to tell you the names of the baby animals for those in the display, such as piglet or lamb.
● What sort of food do the animals eat?
● Talk about the food that we get from farms, such as wheat for bread and milk from cows.

Home links
● Invite a farmer into school to talk to the children about the dangers on a farm. Ask parents and carers to reinforce this message.
● Organize a visit to a farm and ask parents and carers to help.
● Ask an adult to come into the setting to make bread with the children.

Birds

Learning objective: to find out that some animals have feathers and most of these are able to fly.

What you need

Different-coloured tissue paper; an old brown textured towel; grey backing paper; a small cardboard box; a long cardboard tube; white, red green and black paper; white card leaf and bird templates; grey, brown, yellow and green paint; paintbrushes; sponge pieces; brown and green fabric; toothbrushes; glue; scissors; black feathers; non-fiction books; pictures of birds; a net of bird nuts.

What to do

Begin by talking about how birds are different to other animals. What do they have that make them special? Encourage the children to name and describe some birds that they know.

Cover a display board with grey backing paper. Create a tree trunk by stapling a textured towel to the centre of the board. At the top of the trunk, make branches from lighter brown fabric strips, scrunched and shaped to create different shapes and sizes. Ask the children to use toothbrushes to stroke brown paint onto white or black paper and fix these to the trunk and branches to give a textured bark effect.

Draw around the leaf template onto white card to make several leaves. Invite the children to paint or sponge-print them green. When dry, attach them at intervals to the branches. Around the base of the trunk, glue grass made from tall triangular spears of mid and light green tissue paper.

To make birds, glue scrunched-up tissue paper to the bird templates. Use blue and yellow to make the blue tits, brown, white and red for the robins, and brown for the owls. The crows are made from black tissue paper and feathers, bought from a craft shop. Paint the beaks and feet bright yellow. To make a pigeon, cover two templates with scrunched white paper to make a front and back. Use a wide paintbrush to dab grey paint on both sides. When dry, staple the two pieces together three-quarters of the way round, leaving a small space at the breast area. Stuff the pigeon with paper before stapling the space together. Sit the pigeon on the floor in front of the display or, alternatively, attach a piece of thread and suspend it above the tree. Add different birds as desired, depending on those found around your setting.

Paint a small cardboard box and long tube with thick brown paint. When dry,

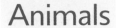

cut a hole in the front of the box then tape it to the top of the tube to make a birdhouse. Place this to one side of the display. Dangle a net of nuts underneath to add effect.

Cover a small table with green fabric and use it to display books, pictures of birds, feathers and children's work. Finally, make a title from letters cut from red paper backed onto green.

Talk about
● Be birdspotters for a day. Talk about the different shapes, sizes and colours of birds that you spot in your area.
● Discuss ways in which birds move, such as walking, paddling or flying. Do all birds move in the same way?
● Why should the children leave nesting sites alone? Reinforce the importance of leaving birds in peace as they nest.

Home links
● Ask a carer or parent if they know anyone who keeps birds who might come in and talk to the children.
● Invite someone into the setting who has young chicks. Follow the policy for your setting on inviting in visitors.
● Organize a visit to a fowl trust or bird sanctuary and invite carers and parents to take part.

Using the display
Language and literacy
● Introduce the language related to birds for example beak, claw, feathers, wing, fly.

Mathematics
● Count the number of legs, eyes, beaks, claws and so on. How many legs on two birds? On three birds?
● Sort pictures of birds by colour and size.

Knowledge and understanding of the world
● Make simple comparisons between ourselves and birds using can/cannot criteria.
● Can all birds fly? Introduce non-flying birds, showing the children pictures from information books. How do these birds move around?

Physical development
● Listen to 'Hens and Cockerels' from *The Carnival of the Animals* by Saint-Saëns. Encourage the children to practise moving around like the different birds, then help them to make up a simple dance sequence to the music.

Animals

Caring for animals

Learning objective: to learn how to care for our pets.

What you need
A display table; a collection of accessories which are needed to care for pets such as a grooming brush, feeding bowls, collars, leads, photocopies of registration documents, toys and food; a piece of deep purple fabric; different-sized cardboard boxes; stapler; non-fiction books; labels; purple and yellow paper; photographs and paintings of the children's pets.

What to do
Ask the children to think about what they need to do in order to look after their pets. Who feeds their pets? Why do they need to be walked and groomed? Tell the children that they are going to help you to make a display which shows the many things that we need in order to look after our pets.

Place the cardboard boxes at intervals on the display table and cover with the deep purple fabric. This will create different levels on which to display the items you have collected. Arrange the items on the table ensuring that they can be seen easily by the children and are well spaced out. Mount the children's photographs and paintings on paper of a complementary colour then display them on the table-top and on the drape at the front of the table. Double mount the labels on purple and yellow paper before placing them in the appropriate places on the display.

Talk about
● Discuss the range of equipment needed for the animals to be well cared for. How are the accessories used?
● Talk about the importance of giving pets plenty of exercise.
● What do animals eat? Do dogs eat the same food as fish? Should we give animals sweets? Why not? This discussion could lead on to talking about how we look after our own bodies, particularly our teeth.

Home links
● Send a letter home to parents and carers asking for relevant items which are safe to handle and meet health and safety requirements.
● If anyone offers to bring in animals for the children to see, ensure that you follow your setting's policy.

Further display table ideas
● Make displays of different types of animals, for example a display of animals which are mammals, insects, reptiles or birds. Include models, toys, pictures and books.
● Make a display of animal masks. Include commercially bought ones with those made by the children.
● Convert your water tray into a pond or sea scene, and your sand tray into a farm or desert, with model animals.

SCIENCE

Growing

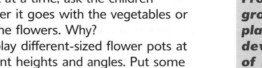
Growing tools

Learning objective: to learn about the tools that are used for growing plants.

What you need
Display board; posters of plants and flowers; empty seed packets; cardboard boxes; green fabric; stapler; a collection of objects used for growing plants.

What to do
Look at the collection of the items with the children. Can they name the items? Tell the children that you are going to use the items to make a display showing things that people use to grow plants.

Arrange the boxes in front of the display board then cover the board and boxes with the green drape. Staple the posters randomly onto the board.

Select two seed packets, one vegetable and one flower. Place one packet on one side of the board and one on the other side. Taking one packet at a time, ask the children whether it goes with the vegetables or with the flowers. Why?

Display different-sized flower pots at different heights and angles. Put some compost in a container and add a watering can full of water.

Talk about
● Discuss the different types of seeds. Which ones will we be able to eat when they have grown?
● Why do plants need compost? Why is the watering can important? Explain that plants need water to grow.
● Plant some seeds and record their growth using a camera. Display the photographs alongside each other.

Home links
● Ask parents and carers to contribute items from home or to buy them from a local garden centre.
● Organize a visit to a garden centre and ask parents and carers to help.

From the growth of plants to the development of babies, this chapter provides opportunities for children to learn about and understand the growing process through a range of lively, interactive displays

Growing

THEMES ON DISPLAY for early years

In the garden

Learning objective: to learn that many plants grow.

What you need

Purple and yellow backing paper; cardboard boxes; yellow and red tissue paper; yellow crêpe paper; paint and brushes; yellow wool; cardboard egg boxes; green garden canes; scraps of yellow, red and orange gummed paper and fabric; dried pulses; green and yellow sugar paper; crayons and felt-tipped pens; A4 white and bright green paper; stapler; PVA glue; sticky tape; scissors; plants and seasonal flowers; models of insects, mammals and birds.

What to do

Over several sessions, involve the children in making flowers using different techniques and materials.

● Make buttercups by painting large heart-shaped petals with thick yellow paint. When dry, coat them with PVA glue. Arrange in a circular pattern. Fringe a circle of yellow tissue paper and glue scrunched-up tissue paper in a slightly darker shade of yellow to this circle. Attach to the centre of the petals.

● To make daisies, ask the children to make white handprints on green sugar paper. Cut out the handprints and glue them in a circle. Make centres by sticking squares of yellow crêpe paper and yellow wool to yellow sugar paper circles using PVA glue.

● To make foxgloves, paint cardboard egg boxes with thick purple paint. Cut green sugar paper stems and glue to sheets of white paper. Cut out segments from the egg boxes and glue to either side of the stems. Cut around the completed shapes.

● Cut out paper circles and ask the children to decorate them using gummed paper, fabric and other paper scraps. Tape the flower heads to garden canes, then wrap paper around the joins to disguise them.

● Give the children flower shape outlines on white paper to colour with wax crayons or felt-tipped pens. Cut these out and attach a green strip of paper for the stem.

● Collage simple flower shapes using tissue paper and glue dried pulses to the centre of the shapes.

To make grass, ask the children to place their hands on a sheet of green paper, with their fingers splayed. Draw and then cut out the outline. Paint small brown tree shapes and let the children add green finger-painted leaves.

Cover the display board in deep purple backing paper and staple the painted branches around the edge. Arrange the flowers on the board and intersperse them with the green 'grass' handprints. Add the learning objective cut from yellow paper.

Place cardboard boxes or wooden blocks covered in purple paper in front of the board. Arrange different varieties of plants – flowering and non-flowering – and pots of flowers across the surface. Hide models of insects and small mammals among the display and suspend models of birds in front.

Talk about
● If possible, take the children outside to look at the different flowers around your setting. If it is summertime, there will probably be lots of daisies, buttercups and dandelions to compare.
● Tell the children that foxgloves are poisonous, and that they should not touch them.

● Talk about other poisonous things, such as seeds and berries. NB: Some seeds are dressed in insecticide – do not use these in your setting.
● Discuss the animals and birds that live among the plants. Which parts of the plants do the birds eat?

Home links
● Invite an adult to help supervise the hand-printing activity, making sure the children roll their hands firmly onto the paper.
● Organize a 'cutting out' club one morning to support the children and to model the cutting out of more difficult shapes for them.

Using the display
Personal, social and emotional development
● Talk about how to care for plants so that they grow properly. Invite the children to suggest all the things that a plant needs in order to grow.
● Remind the children that they must not pick flowers.

Language and literacy
● Develop the role-play area into a garden centre to teach the language of plants and flowers.
● Read stories and rhymes about growing such as *The Tiny Seed* by Eric Carle (Puffin) and *Titch* by Pat Hutchins (Red Fox).
● Make up a group poem using the display as a stimulus.

Mathematics
● Talk about the sizes and shapes of the plants and flowers. What shape are the petals? Which is the tallest plant?

Knowledge and understanding of the world
● Teach the children the names of

the flowers that have been used in the display. Are they found in the gardens near the school or do the flowers come from another country?
● Compare two plants. Make a list of the things which are the same, for example, the leaves on both plants are green, they both have roots; and the things which are different, for example, the leaves are a different shape, the stems are a different thickness.

Physical development
● There are lots of opportunities to develop the children's cutting and colouring skills in the flower-making activities.

Creative development
● Invite the children to design their own flowers using crayons, paint and collage.
● Sing rhymes and songs with the children about gardens, such as 'Mary, Mary, Quite Contrary'; 'One Potato, Two Potato' and 'This is the Way to Dig (Weed, Plant...) the Garden' to the tune of 'Here We Go Round the Mulberry Bush'.

A flower

Learning objective: to learn that flowers have roots, a stem, petals and leaves.

What you need

A tall display board; purple backing paper; yellow letters; chalk; strips of green card; large squares of white cotton cloth; nettles, grass, onion skins and red cabbage; three saucepans; a cooker in a safe area; water; a good quantity of salt; a washing line in an open area; stapler; string; labels for roots, flower, leaves and stem; information books with clear pictures showing all parts of a plant.

What to do

Gather the children together and share the information books. Talk about the different plants of a flower, and show examples if possible. Now explain that you are going to make a picture of a large flower showing the roots, leaves, stem and petals.

Show the children the white cotton squares and explain that you are going to use different parts of plants to change their colour. Tell them that this process is called dyeing.

Show the children the onion skins and ask them if they know what they are. Confirm that they are onion skins and then tell the children that you are going to boil them in water, together with some of the cotton squares, and that this will change the colour of the cloth.

Use twelve squares of cloth – four for the centre of the flower and eight to make four of the petals. Can the children guess what colour the squares will become? Boil the skins with the squares until you are happy with the depth of colour. They should turn yellowy-orange. Plunge the squares into cold water mixed with a strong solution of salt to fix the dye and then hang on a washing line to dry.

Next, show the children the nettles and grass. You will need enough squares to make two leaves and a long stem. Repeat the activity and boil the squares until you have the required shade of green. Use the red cabbage and eight squares to make four reddish petals.

Cover the display board with purple paper and staple the green card strips in ripples around the edge to

SCIENCE

Using the display
Personal, social and emotional development
●Talk about the children's favourite flowers. Invite them to use pictures cut from magazines and their own drawings to make cards for their friends.

Language and literacy
●Go on a 'Flower walk' around your setting and name all the flowers that you see.
●Read a story about growing a plant such as *Rachel's Roses* by Karen Christensen (Barefoot Books).

Mathematics
●Count the number of petals in your flower. Can you find flowers with the same number of petals? Can you find flowers with more and fewer petals?

Knowledge and understanding of the world
●Bring in different kinds of flowers and talk about their similarities and differences.
●Use a paint or draw program, such as *TinyArt* (Topologika) on the computer for the children to draw their own flowers. Demonstrate how to change the size of the paintbrush to paint the roots and stem; and change the colours for the leaves, stem, roots and petals.

Creative development
●Use commercial dyes to dye cotton squares in different colours. Invite the children to use fabric pens to draw flowers onto plain cotton squares. Sew the squares together, or mount them on the wall, to make a patchwork pattern.

make a border. Use chalk to draw a faint outline of a large flower with eight petals on the board. Shape eight of the red squares into four petals, and eight orange squares into four petals and staple into position. Scrunch the yellow squares into interesting shapes and staple to the board to form the centre of the flower.

Roll several green squares into cylinder shapes and staple these below the flower to form the stem. Shape the remaining green squares into leaf shapes and attach to the bottom at either side of the stem. Attach small lengths of string to the bottom of the stem for the root system.

Finally, add the title 'Flowers have many different parts' made from letters cut from yellow paper. Ask the children to help you place the labels in the appropriate places.

Talk about
●Encourage the children to think about the difference between wild flowers and garden flowers. Discuss the wild flowers, which are protected because they are in danger of disappearing.
●Talk about the different colours that the dyeing process produced. Can the children suggest other items to use to dye the fabric in different colours?

Home links
●Ask carers and parents to contribute items with flowers in their design to make a tabletop display.
●Encourage carers and parents to point out the parts of other plants in the environment, for example a tree has a trunk, roots, branches, twigs and leaves.

Growing

THEMES ON DISPLAY
for early years

Jack and the beanstalk

Learning objective: to learn that plants grow from seeds.

What you need
Two display boards and a ceiling; white and green backing paper; newspaper; brown, green, pink, black and red paint; black and yellow wool; blue fabric; hay; white candles or wax crayons; foil papers; old net curtains; green, yellow and pink Cellophane; white card; black and yellow sugar paper; scissors; rectangles of white paper; PVA glue; stapler.

What to do
Begin by reading the story of 'Jack and the Beanstalk' (traditional). Talk about the beanstalk. What did it grow from? Do beanstalks really grow that tall? Invite the children to help you to make a display which shows how plants grow from seeds.

Cut large leaf shapes from white card. Support the children to use white candles or crayons to mark leaf veins onto the templates. They will need to press very hard. Make a colour wash with green powder paint and let the children give the leaves a light covering.

To make this display you will need two display boards – one for Jack's house and one for the giant's castle – plus another area on which to mount the giant. The areas will be linked by the beanstalk. Begin by making the castle.

Cover one of the display boards in green backing paper. To make the beanstalk, roll several sheets of newspaper into tight cylinder shapes and paint them with thick brown paint. Attach the beanstalk up the display board and across the ceiling towards the other display board. Staple the leaves along the beanstalk at intervals.

To make the castle, invite the children to help you cover rectangles of white paper with scraps of foil paper. The display is particularly effective if you stick to one colour scheme, such as purple. Paint any gaps with red paint. When dry, staple the sheets to the display board into the shape of a castle, cutting into shape where necessary.

Make arched windows and a door from green and pink Cellophane, respectively. To make the display more interesting, make a border for the windows from red foil sweet dishes and use blue ones for the door.

To make the giant, draw around an adult onto a large sheet of paper. Paint in a red shirt, brown trousers and black boots. Paint the giant's face pink, and invite the children to help to glue on black wool to make hair and a beard. Mount the giant on the wall near the castle.

Make the cottage by stapling sheets of white rectangular paper to the second display board in the shape of a cottage. Add strips of black paper to represent beams. Cut out the shape of a roof from yellow sugar paper and cover it liberally with PVA glue. Invite the children to press the hay firmly onto the glue to make a thatched roof. Make the windows by covering two sheets of white paper with yellow Cellophane. Create a lattice effect by gluing strips of black sugar paper across the windows in diagonal lines. Add strips of white net to look like curtains. Paint a large sheet of paper brown and add black hinges and bolts to make it look like a door. Staple this into position.

Join all three parts of the display by adding more sections of beanstalk and leaves.

To make Jack, draw around the outline of a child. Ask the children to stick on blue fabric scraps to make his shirt and trousers. Finally, glue on yellow wool for hair.

Add the title in yellow lettering underneath the giant's castle.

Talk about
● Discuss the story with the children. Do they think it was a good idea for Jack to sell the cow for a few beans?

Using the display
Language and literacy
● Act out the story of 'Jack and the Beanstalk'. Encourage the children to use different voices to depict different characters.

Mathematics
● Develop the language of comparative size by comparing the size of the characters in the story. Who is the tallest/largest/fattest/shortest? Who is taller than Jack, shorter than the giant, larger than Jack's mother?
● Jack was given five beans in exchange for his cow. Sing some counting rhymes involving the number five such as 'Five little speckled frogs' or 'Five little ducks'.

Knowledge and understanding of the world
● Plant bean seeds in glass jars lined with absorbent paper. Encourage the children to follow the progress of the seeds as they develop roots and leaves. Place the seedlings on a table in front of the display to reinforce the learning objective.
● Plant some bean seeds in grow bags. Suspend string for the beans to climb up. Record the growth with a digital camera and display the photographs alongside each other to illustrate the growing sequence.

Creative development
● Encourage the children to paint their own pictures of Jack and the Beanstalk.

What would they have done?
● Was it brave of Jack to go to the giant's castle? Use this opportunity to talk about 'stranger danger'.

Home links
● Invite carers and parents to support the children making the leaves for the beanstalk, rolling the newspapers for the stems and attaching the hay for the roof of Jack's house.

Growing

THEMES ON DISPLAY
for early years

Corn in the fields

Learning objective: to learn that people grow lots of things to eat.

What you need

Green and red backing paper; a large sheet of white paper; 5cm square sponge blocks; blue, red, black, yellow, pink and dark and light brown paint; black and brown fabric; PVA glue; stapler; scissors; cotton wool; fluorescent yellow card; yellow wool; wheat; red fabric poppies; pictures of fruit and vegetables being grown; items of food that are grown.

What to do

Show the children the pictures of the food being grown. Who grows the food? What happens to it after it is picked? Invite the children to examine the wheat. Can they name anything that is made from wheat? Tell the children that you are going to make a display which shows some of the different foods that people grow for us to eat.

Invite the children to sponge-print several yellow, red and blue squares. Let the children cut these out themselves when they are dry. Draw and cut out the shape of a scarecrow from a large sheet of white paper. Ask the children to glue the red and yellow squares to his jacket and blue squares to his hat. Add a few blue squares to make patches. Paint the scarecrow's face and add eyes and a smiley mouth.

Cover a display board with green backing paper. Across the bottom third of the board attach strips of earth made by printing white paper with sponge squares dipped in dark brown paint. When dry, add to the texture by printing another layer with light brown or pink paint. Paint in black rabbits' burrows. Staple the scarecrow to the board.

Ask the children to draw pictures of rabbits, then glue on squares of brown and black fabric to give them texture. Add cotton wool tails. Cut out the rabbits and staple some below ground. Above the ground and around the scarecrow, staple the wheat and red poppies.

Cut out shapes of ears of corn from fluorescent yellow card. Invite the children to fill the sections with yellow wool curled into spirals. Staple the completed pieces of wheat around the edge of the picture to form a border. Add the title cut from red lettering. In front of the picture, display the collection of fruits and vegetables.

Talk about
● Discuss the foods grown in your local area, particularly if you live in a farming or market gardening area.
● Visit your local supermarket or greengrocer to look at the variety of food which has been grown. Some more able children may be able to discuss which have been grown in this country and which have been grown abroad.
●Make a collection of all the food items that are made from wheat.

Home links
●Ask among your parents or carers whether anyone grows their own food. Invite them in to talk to the children, showing examples if possible. Make sure that you follow your setting's policy for inviting visitors.

Using the display
Personal, social and emotional development
●Discuss the importance of food and how we need to eat and drink to stay alive.
●Read the story about Jesus and the loaves and fishes.

Language and literacy
●Introduce the children to new vocabulary, such as the names of fruits and vegetables and the people who grow and sell them.
●Read the story of 'The Little Red Hen' (traditional). Discuss the morals in the story.
●Develop a fruit and vegetable shop in your role-play area. Make fruit and vegetables from play dough or use plastic ones.

Mathematics
●Sort items into sets using different criteria such as fruit and vegetables; colours; big and little; made from wheat and so on.

Knowledge and understanding of the world
●Cut some of the fruits and vegetables in half and look at what is inside. Can the children see the seeds? How many seeds are there? Pumpkin, melon or marrow are particularly good food items to use for this activity.
●Invite the children to complete the photocopiable sheet on page 74. Ask them to colour in the pictures and then carefully cut them out. Help them to put them into the correct order to show the sequence involved in making bread.
●Talk about healthy diets. Let the children help you to make a fruit salad to enjoy during the session. Remember to check with parents and carers for food allergies first.

Physical development
●Develop the children's fine motor skills by giving them plenty of opportunities to practise cutting independently.
●Develop a movement sequence to the theme of 'Growing', from a small shape to a large shape. Introduce simple benches and table apparatus which encourage the children to move at various heights.

Creative development
●Teach the children the rhymes 'Oats and beans and barley grow' and 'Big floppy scarecrows dangling along', both from *This Little Puffin* edited by Elizabeth Matterson (Puffin).

SCIENCE

Taking the baby for a walk

Learning objective: to understand that we all grow.

What you need
Two tables of different heights; green backing paper; strips of red card; paint in a variety of colours including various skin tones and pastel colours; white paper; red felt; yellow ribbon; white and yellow doilies; green tissue paper; squares of fabric in a variety of colours; pieces of wool; PVA glue; stapler; paintbrushes; felt-tipped pens; red paper; a collection of baby toys and equipment brought in by the children; two baby blankets; a small selection of baby and adult clothes.

What to do
Begin by showing the children the baby clothes. Talk about how small a baby is when it is born. Hold the baby clothes up against one of the children. Would they fit into the clothes now? Why not? Now show them the adult clothes and discuss the differences between the two sets of clothes. Talk about growing bigger as we get older, and reinforce the concept by inviting the children to compare themselves to you to highlight the differences. Tell the children that they are going to help you to put together a display which shows how we grow as we get older.

Give each child a sheet of white paper and provide ready-mixed paint in a range of skin tones. Ask the children to paint pictures of themselves as babies. When the pictures are dry, cut them out and glue them to strips of red card. Cover a display board with green paper and staple the children's pictures around the edge to make a border.

Glue green tissue paper spears across the bottom of the board. Invite some children to paint houses in various pastel colours or to draw and colour them using felt-tipped pens. Cut the houses out and staple them across the top of the board to make a street.

Draw and cut out an outline of a pram. Paint the pram red and make a frill by gluing a white doily, cut into strips, around the frame. Arrange the yellow doilies and glue yellow ribbon around the edge of a rectangle of red felt. Glue this into place inside the pram. Add one of the children's baby paintings, then staple the pram to the display board.

Make some family members to add to the scene. Include a child, Mum or Dad and Grandma or Grandad. Draw around different people in your setting to produce the outlines, then invite the children to glue pieces of fabric in a variety of colours to make the clothes. Add hair to the characters by gluing on pieces of wool.

Place two tables of different heights in front of the display and cover them each with a baby's blanket.

On each table display a variety of baby objects which have been brought in by the children.

Finally, add the title 'We all grow' from letters cut from red paper.

Talk about
● Discuss how you have all grown. Show the children a photograph of yourself as a baby, a child and a young adult and compare them to show how much you have grown!
● Talk about the difference in the children's heights, being sure to treat this sensitively. Who is the tallest?

Home links
● Ask carers and parents to send in photographs of the children when they were babies. Set up a 'Guess the baby' competition.
● Ask carers and parents to contribute to the display by sending in items of baby toys and equipment.

Using the display
Personal, social and emotional development
● Make personal record books with the children. Include photographs and drawings of the children from new-born babies to the present day. Talk about how they have changed.

Language and literacy
● Develop the language of growth including grow, big, bigger, biggest, tall, taller, tallest, short, shorter, shortest, heavy, heavier, heaviest.

Mathematics
● Measure the height of each child a term before you intend to set up the display. Measure them again when you work on the display. How much have they grown?
● Use strips of paper to make a growing chart on the wall. Mark the children's heights over a period of time.

Knowledge and understanding of the world
● Make a collection of photographs and sort them into children and adults.

Physical development
● Discuss the things that the children could do when they were a baby, and the things that they can do now. Make a chart to show how much they have learned.

THEMES ON DISPLAY for early years

Lots of things grow

Learning objective: to understand that lots of things grow.

What you need
A display surface; large piece of purple fabric; cardboard boxes of different sizes; a collection of items which have all grown or which are still growing including plants, flowers, vegetables, photographs of people, pictures of animals and reference books of living things; labels; yellow and purple letters; green card.

What to do
Arrange the cardboard boxes across the table-top to produce surfaces of different heights, then cover the area with the purple fabric. Sort the items into sets and arrange them across the display surface. Add labels, photographs and books. Mount the yellow and purple letters for the title to a rectangle of green card and secure across the front of the display.

Talk about
● Discuss the items in your display. Do all living things grow?
● Walk around the setting and ask the

children to help you to identify all the things that grow. On your return to the setting, record all the things that you have found.

Home links
● Ask parents and carers to send in items for the display such as models of animals, photographs of themselves and so on.
● Ask some carers and parents to come along to help with the walk around the setting and the subsequent discussions and recording.
● Give parents and carers a copy of the photocopiable sheet on page 75. Ask them to help their child colour in and cut out the pictures then sort them into sets according to whether they are babies or fully grown.

Further display table ideas
● In springtime, display a selection of flowers which have been grown from bulbs. Incorporate vases of daffodils, tulips and crocuses into the display.
● Display a collection of photographs of people at different ages.
● Display pictures and models of baby animals next to pictures and models of adult animals. Compare their sizes and other differences.

Water

Waterfall

Learning objective: to discover that water is a liquid and spreads if it is not contained.

What you need
Long length of string or ribbon; a range of blue and green papers including crêpe, foil, Cellophane and tissue; silver foil strips; shiny wrapping paper; stapler.

What to do
Cut the paper and foil into strips and staple them to the string or ribbon. Vary the shades of blues and greens and intersperse with silver foil strips and shiny wrapping paper to create a shimmering effect. Hang the length of string or ribbon with the attached streamers across the ceiling so that they hang down to the floor like a curtain. If possible, hang the waterfall in front of a window or other safe draught source, so that they move in the breeze. Tie back the waterfall each day so that you can carry on with your activities as usual.

Talk about
● Talk about how water spreads out if it doesn't have something to stop it. Pour some water slowly into the water tray to demonstrate. Explain that the tray is a container – it contains the water.
● Does water always make the shape of the container that it is in? Let the children investigate by pouring it into a variety of different-shaped containers.
● Invite the children to use their senses to talk about water. What does it feel like? Can they hold it in their hands? Does it have a smell? What colour is it? What sounds does it make when poured?
● Discuss the properties of water. Encourage descriptive language such as wet, damp, liquid, clear, see-through.

Home links
● Send a letter home explaining that you are exploring the properties of water. Ask them to investigate water at bath times.
● Give parents a word list as a prompt to develop children's language.
● Ask parents to visit the local library and book shops to find books suitable for young children.

From a shimmering waterfall to a mass of colourful bubbles, this chapter contains some stunning display ideas on the theme of water, which are guaranteed to bring a splash of colour to your room

Water all around us

Learning objective: to discover that water has many uses.

What you need
A display board and surface; blue backing paper; black sugar paper; pencil; washing line; small items of clothing; wooden and plastic pegs; green, brown red and yellow paint, PVA glue, stapler; scissors; blue Cellophane; yellow and white paper; marker pen; green fabric and wool; black and white felt; sponge.

What to do
Cover the display board with blue paper. Make a border using black sugar paper, rippling it for an interesting effect. Draw a feint line across the background to show where the sky and grass sections will be, and draw the outline of a flowerbed on the left-hand side.

Explain to the children that they are going to help you make a display of a garden to show some of the ways that water is used. The following activities can be divided between morning and afternoon sessions if you wish. Show one group of children how to use a sponge to apply green paint across the bottom of the board to make a lawn. Invite another group to paint the flowerbed brown to form the soil. Leave the top blue for the sky.

Ask a small group of children to paint some colourful flowers on sheets of A4 white paper. When the flowers are dry, cut around the outline and stick some onto the display in the flowerbed.

Ask another group of children to help you make the paddling pool. Provide sheets of paper and yellow paint, and ask the children to paint the sheets. When they are dry, coat the sheets with PVA glue to give a shiny effect. Leave the sheets to dry, then roll them up and staple them onto the grass at the bottom of the display in a rectangular shape. Fill the space with scrunched-up pieces of blue Cellophane paper to represent water.

Cut out the outline of a watering can from sugar paper. Ask one child to paint

SCIENCE

the outline red, then add holes for the water to flow through. Staple the watering can to the board next to the flower bed. Paint two posts at either side of the board and attach the length of washing line to the top of each post.

Cut out some cloud shapes and add texture using curled pieces of white paper which have been dragged firmly across a pair of closed scissors or wrapped around a pencil. Staple the clouds to the sky section.

Make grass from triangular sugar paper spears covered in a variety of shades of green fabric squares and wool. Staple these to the sponge painted lawn, and add the rest of the children's painted flowers.

Make five stepping stones leading up to the display using circles of black felt. Cut five smaller circles from white felt and number them from one to five. Glue these on top of the larger circles.

Gather the children together in front of the display. Hold up a pair of socks and explain that you are going to hang these on the washing line. Ask the children whereabouts on the line they would like you to hang the socks. Continue in this way until all the clothes have been hung on the line.

To complete the display, mount the words 'Water is used for' across the top of the board.

Talk about
● Talk about the different things that we use water for. Invite the children to draw a picture of one thing that they use water for and to write a simple label.
● Talk about favourite drinks. Do the children like to drink water? Do they need to add water to their favourite drink?
● What happens when we add things to water? Talk about how it changes colour, goes frothy, gets dirty and so on.
● Talk about the dangers of water, such as scalding from hot taps or drowning.

Home links
● Encourage one or two parents to come in and help the children with the sponge painting and cutting out activities.
● Send a letter home to explain that you will be talking about the dangers of water for parents to reinforce at home.

watering can

Using the display
Personal, social and emotional development
● Set up an activity in the role-play area for the children to wash up the crockery and wash the dolls' clothes.

Language and literacy
● Invite the children to draw a picture of themselves using water at home. Ask them to describe what they are doing, and scribe their comments for them.
● Sing songs and nursery rhymes such as 'Mary, Mary, Quite Contrary' and 'Jack and Jill'.

Mathematics
● Make a pictogram of the children's favourite drinks.
● Change the number of pegs and items on the washing line each day and use these for counting activities.
● Sort the pegs into sets according to colour, material, size and texture.
● Use the numbered stepping stones for counting games.

Knowledge and understanding of the world
● Talk about water in your area – it could be a lake, a river, the seaside or pond in the local environment.
● Make ice lollies and jellies to show how water changes through heating and freezing.

Bubbles

Learning objective: to find out that bubbles can be made from soapy water.

What you need
Coloured backing paper; paint pots containing different coloured paints; washing-up liquid; straws; A4 absorbent paper; scissors; shallow tray; oil-based marbling paints or cooking oil and food colouring; water; stapler; thread; display table; coloured fabric; bubble-blowing equipment.

What to do
Cover a display board with a colour of your choice. Show the children the pots containing the different coloured paints and, while they are watching, add a small amount of washing-up liquid to each pot. Ask the children to say what they think will happen if you blow through the straw into the pot. Blow into the pot until you have a mound of bubbles appearing over the top. This will cause great excitement!

Place a sheet of A4 paper onto the bubbles and press down. Carefully lift the paper away to show the children the pattern you have made. Invite them to have a go at making their own bubble patterns, providing plenty of support. When dry, carefully draw circle shapes around the bubble patterns and encourage the children to cut them out. Cut out some yourself to ensure that there are a few accurate circles.

Make different bubble shapes using a marbling technique. Add water and oil based marbling paints to a shallow tray. Alternatively, use cooking oil and food colouring. Swirl the oil and water together to make a beautiful pattern, then carefully drop a sheet of A4 absorbent paper onto the surface. Remove the paper and show the children the pattern you have made.

Help the children to make their own patterns. Again, when dry, draw circles around the patterns and cut them out carefully. Staple the circles together onto the display board to create a giant bubble.

Attach more bubbles around the outside of the display to make a border. Stick some bubbles back to back and attach thread to make colourful mobiles. Suspend these from the ceiling in front of the display. Add the title 'Bubbles', written in bubble lettering.

Cover a table with fabric and place it in front of the display. Place different bubble blowers and a bubble mixture for the children to use.

Talk about
● Talk about the shapes

SCIENCE

of the bubbles. What colours can the children see? Can they see their own reflection?
● What happens when you blow into the paint mixture?
● Remind the children that you added washing-up liquid to the water before you blew the bubbles. How is washing-up liquid used at home?
● Talk about the dangers of handling other household cleaners. Make a collection of pictures which show 'unsafe to touch' items in the kitchen.

Home links
● Ask parents to come in to help the children cut out their circle shapes, to supervise the bubble blowing and to encourage the children to take turns and share the bubble blowers.

Bubbles

Bubbles here, bubbles there,
Bubbles floating everywhere.
Some go high, some go low
We don't know just where they go.
Pretty colours floating by
Going high into the sky.
And, Oh I'm sad when they go POP!
I wish that they would never stop.

Using the display
Personal, social and emotional development
● Take turns to blow bubbles using the range of bubble blowers included in the display.
● Add washing flakes or bubble bath mixture to the water tray and encourage the children to make as many bubbles as they can. How many bubbles can they hold in their hand? Can they work with a partner to make bubble sculptures?

Language and literacy
● Make a list of words to describe the bubbles. Introduce the names of the colours that can be seen in the bubbles, as well as words such as transparent, reflection and see through. Make labels and add them to the display.
● Write a poem to describe the way that bubbles move. Model the writing with the children.

Mathematics
● Make a collection of circles and use them to make a display. Use this as a starting point to extend into discussing the names of other shapes.
● Develop the language of size. Blow two bubbles and ask the children to point out the bigger one, smaller one and so on.
● Teach the children a counting song about bubbles to the tune of 'Here We Go Round The Mulberry Bush'.

Physical development
● Develop early pencil control skills by making circle picture and pattern sheets for the children to trace.
● Draw circles in clockwise and anti-clockwise movements to develop hand/eye co-ordination skills.
● During PE, develop the theme of moving in a circle.

Five little bubbles floating around,
Floating around, floating around.
One little bubble floats down to the ground
And that little bubble goes POP!
Four little bubbles... *and so on*

Rain and shine

Learning objective: to understand that water falls from the sky as rain.

What you need
Blue backing paper; sugar paper; paint in various colours; thick-bristled brush; red, orange, yellow, green, blue, purple and violet tissue paper; cold water paste; silver and pale blue paper; a large sponge; small pieces of sponge; scissors; stapler; pinking shears; blue sequin strip; pieces of paper or newspaper.

What to do
Cover the display board with blue backing paper. Draw and cut out a simple outline of a small person from sugar paper. The person should be dressed in a raincoat, mittens and wellington boots. Give the person a raised arm and draw in the handle of an umbrella.

In small groups, ask the children to paint the raincoat yellow, the wellington boots red and the handle of the umbrella brown. When the paint has dried, ask another group to paint in the facial features and cover the mittens with scrunched-up tissue paper in a colour of their choice.

Ask another group of children to make a rainbow. Cut out a large arc from the sugar paper and divide it into seven strips of equal widths. Cover the paper with cold water paste and invite the children to fill in the strips with scrunched-up tissue paper in the colours of the rainbow: red, orange, yellow, green, blue, purple and violet.

Cut a large cloud outline from the sugar paper and invite the children to help you to glue on scrunched-up newspaper or waste paper. When dry, turn the cloud into a dark grey raincloud by dabbing on grey and white paint with a thick bristled brush. Cut out the outline of the sun, and add flat, yellow tissue paper squares. Make a large puddle from silver paper, crumpled to look like water.

To make the umbrella, cut out a large circle from sugar paper. Divide the circle into sections to look like the separate sections of an umbrella and cut a curved

SCIENCE

edge between each one, so it looks as if the umbrella is open. Let the children choose which colours they would like to use to paint the umbrella, then leave to one side to dry.

Attach the sun to the display board, followed by the rainbow and then the cloud, so that the sun and rainbow are peeping out from either side of the cloud. Attach the person in front, leaving the feet unattached. Slot the puddle in underneath the feet and secure both in place. Add small ovals of silver paper above the puddle to look like splashes of water.

Fold the umbrella shape in half, so you have a semicircle shape. Staple the back of the semicircle to the display board. Attach a large sponge to the centre of the semicircle, underneath. The sponge will lift the front section of the umbrella away from the wall, creating a three-dimensional effect.

Ask the children to make cloud and raindrop mobiles to hang in front of the display by sponge painting small cut-out clouds with grey paint, and cutting out raindrop shapes from blue paper using pinking shears. Finally, drape a twisted, blue sequin strip from the ceiling, to one side and in front of the display.

To complete the display, add the poem 'Rain, rain, go away' and a title 'Rainy days' using lettering cut from silver paper.

Talk about
● On a rainy day, invite the children to look at the dark clouds in the sky. What shapes are they? Are they all one colour? Invite the children to describe what they think the clouds would feel like if they could touch them.
● What happens when it rains? Explain to the children that the water comes from the clouds.
● What clothes do we wear when it rains? What materials are they made from? How does an umbrella keep us dry on a rainy day?

Home links
● Ask carers to talk to the children about rainbows. If there is an opportunity, look for a rainbow in the sky, or make one outside using a hosepipe on a sunny day. Ask them to reinforce the colours of the rainbow.

Using the display
Language and literacy
● Talk about the word 'waterproof'. What does it mean? Do the children own any waterproof clothing?

Knowledge and understanding of the world
● Talk about rainbows. Explain that we see a rainbow usually when it rains and the sun is shining at the same time.
● Keep a tally chart to record the number of rainy days in each month. Let the children count up the marks to work out which week was the rainiest.

Creative development
● Teach the children the songs 'I Hear Thunder' and 'Rain, Rain, Go Away'.
● Choose a suitable poem about rain and add a simple percussive accompaniment to depict the sound of the rain.

SCIENCE

Pondlife

Learning objective: to learn that some creatures live in a pond.

What you need
Blue backing paper, green Cellophane and foil paper; bubble wrap; brown and green fabric; garden canes; sticky tape; stapler; black and bright green paint; green wax crayons; black felt-tipped pens; large leaves; chicken wire; cutters; newspaper; red and yellow pastels; A4 white and pastel coloured sugar paper; shiny green paper; sequins; glue; water-based paste; coloured tissue paper; tissues; information books and stories about creatures who live in ponds.

What to do
The separate elements of this display can be made over several days with different groups. Cover a board with blue backing paper, then staple green Cellophane paper across the bottom half to make a pond.

Invite some of the children to make bulrushes. Cut spears from green foil paper and staple to the board at either side of the pond. Cut out oval shapes to make the heads of the bulrushes then invite the children to collage them with small squares of brown fabric. Attach the completed heads to green garden canes using sticky tape. Staple them among the leaves, at different heights.

At the bottom of the pond, create frogspawn using bubble wrap. Ask a small group of children to paint black dots onto the bubble wrap to represent the eggs. Invite the children to use black felt-tipped pens to draw pictures of tadpoles on white paper. Cut these out and glue them to the Cellophane.

Ask another group to make frogs. Provide outlines and invite the children to stick on green papers and fabrics. Add eyes made from shiny green paper and sequins. Work with another group to cut out stones for the frogs to sit on. Let the children cut shapes from pale sugar paper, then invite them to use red and yellow soft pastels to colour the shapes. Use a tissue to blend the pastels.

Collect large green leaves with the children. Using a range of greens, make wax crayon rubbings of the leaves on white paper, then cut them out and glue them to the top of the pond.

Add some colourful dragonflies sculptured with chicken wire. Carefully cut off a length of chicken wire and squeeze it into a cylindrical shape. Make one end fatter, for the head and the other end pointed, for the tail. Make sure all the sharp edges are inside the sculpture. Weave strips of newspaper in and out of the wire to make a base for the papier mâché. Show the children how to cover the frame with several layers of paper using a thick water-based paste. Make sure that you do not use one that contains an insect repellent. Use white paper for the last layer as it will take paint better than newspaper. When the paper layers have set, paint the sculpture bright green. Make wings from wire covered with colourful tissue paper and attach to the body with another length of wire. Attach to the display with staples.

Talk about
● Look at information and story books about pond creatures. Talk about other creatures that live in ponds that have not been included in the display.
● Talk about the dangers of going near water without an adult.
● Talk about why it is important that creatures are not taken from their natural habitat, emphasizing the fact that creatures often die if they are taken away from their natural environments.

Home links
● Use an adult helper to help supervise the children in the collection of leaves. Follow your setting's guidelines for taking children outside.
● Ask if any parent has a pond in their garden that is safe for the children to visit. Alternatively, there may be one nearby which is designated by your local authority as a safe place for young children to visit. Ensure additional adult support is available.

Using the display
Personal, social and emotional development
● Develop the sense of what is right and wrong, and our responsibility to take care of living creatures and our environment.

Language and literacy
● Develop the vocabulary of similarities and differences by comparing a picture of a frog and a dragonfly.

Mathematics
● Learn the rhyme 'Five Little Speckled Frogs'.

Knowledge and understanding of the world
● Talk about the life cycle of a frog.

Physical development
● Introduce jumping as a theme for gross motor skill development.
● Develop 'Jumping frog' handwriting sheets for the children to trace and continue in order to develop fine motor skills.

Sealife

Learning objective: to find out that some creatures live in the sea.

What you need
Blue backing paper; four pairs of flesh-coloured tights; green cold water dye; wide range of different shades of green paper and paint; card; PVA glue; egg boxes; silver foil circular tray; silver paper; fluorescent, brown, orange and black paint; blue papers and fabrics; black paper; split pins; a selection of picture books about creatures that live in the sea.

What to do
Cover your chosen display board with blue backing paper. Gather the children together and tell them that you are going to make a picture of some of the creatures that live in the sea. Show them the books and together choose the creatures that the children would like to include.

Begin by making a giant octopus. Dye four pairs of flesh-coloured tights green, using a cold water dye. Don't worry if the dye takes unevenly, as this will add to the effect. Ask the children to screw up scraps, or fold strips, of different shades of green paper like a concertina. When the tights are dry, stuff the legs with the green paper, leaving one pair of tights smaller than the rest so that the tentacles can be graduated. Paint black spots along each leg to look like suckers.

To make the head and body of the octopus, cut out a large oval piece of card and paint it green. While it is drying, invite the children to paint segments of cardboard eggboxes using darker green paint. When the paint is dry, glue the upturned segments all over the octopus's body. Finish off the head by attaching a single eye made from a foil circular tray, adding a blue eyeball in the centre. Finally, staple the head into place on the wall in a prominent position and attach the tentacles so that they stretch in all directions.

Make some fish by cutting simple outlines from card and painting them in bright colours. Invite the children to stick on colourful foil spots.

Cut out some crab outlines from card and ask the children to paint them using shades of brown and orange. Paint over with PVA glue to create a shiny effect. Some children may be able, with adult help, to make moveable crabs legs by joining sections of card with split pins. Make a rock pool for the crabs from scrunched-up black paper and attach this to the bottom of the display before adding the crabs.

Invite suggestions from the

SCIENCE

children about other creatures to add to the display. Ask a small group to work together to make collage dolphins, providing ready-cut outlines and scraps of silver paper. Provide starfish and seahorse outlines for the children to paint and decorate with brown finger-print dots.

Talk about
● Discuss the different creatures that live in the sea. Talk about similarities and differences, whether they have legs, fins, eyes, mouths, ears and so on.
● Compare the octopus to ourselves. How is it like us? How is it different? Tell the children that the correct word for the octopus's legs is tentacles.

Home links
● Ask parents to help with the difficult skills required to make this display, such as folding the paper and stuffing the tentacles, making the crab's legs and cutting out the eggbox sections.

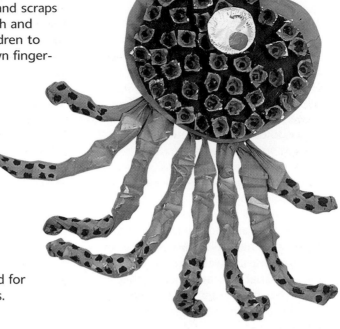

● Organize a visit to a sealife centre. Ask carers to help, or alternatively, invite all carers to join in.

Using the display
Personal, social and emotional development
● Tell the children the story about Jonah and the Whale.

Language and literacy
● Introduce language pertinent to the display such as tentacles, salt water, fins and gills.

Mathematics
● Find different numbers in the display, for example, the octopus has one eye, the crabs have two eyes, the starfish have five legs, the octopus has eight tentacles.

Knowledge and understanding of the world
● Show the children a globe and talk about how the earth is made up of land and sea. Which bits do they think is the land? Why? Point out how much sea there is in the world. Some children may be able to tell you the name of some seas and oceans.
● Take the children to a local fishmongers or supermarket to look at the variety of food we get from the sea.
● Use a CD-ROM to find information about the creatures who live in the sea. 'Magic School Bus: Oceans' (Microsoft) is aimed at pupils aged six and over, but can be used with adult support to investigate life under the sea.

Creative development
● Give the children a copy of the photocopiable sheet on page 76 and invite them to decorate the fish using colourful pens or paints. Add these to the display.

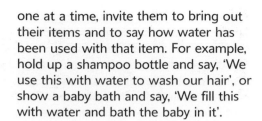
Buckets, bottles and things

Learning objective: to learn about the things which hold and use water.

What you need

A table or cupboard top; blue paper or fabric; card; felt-tipped pen; a collection of items which are used with water such as a bucket, shampoo, bubble bath, flannel, sponge, towel.

What to do

This table-top display is an extension of the 'Water all around us' display. Gather the children around the picture and tell them that the display shows three different uses of water. Can the children tell you what they are? Explain that water has been used for washing clothes, watering plants and filling up a paddling pool.

Tell the children that you would like them to help you make a display which shows items that use water. Show them a flannel, sponge and towel and ask them if they know how these items are used with water. Encourage them to suggest that we use these things to wash or have a bath. Praise the children and invite them to suggest other things that are used with water.

Explain that you would like the children to bring in some items which are used with water to add to the display. On the designated day, gather the children in front of the display and, one at a time, invite them to bring out their items and to say how water has been used with that item. For example, hold up a shampoo bottle and say, 'We use this with water to wash our hair', or show a baby bath and say, 'We fill this with water and bath the baby in it'.

Talk about

● Can the children think of any other ways that water is used with the items. For example, they might suggest that we use a hosepipe to water the garden and to clean the car.

● Talk about the different ways in which you could sort the items, for example those used for cleaning, drinking or playing.

Home links

● Send a letter to parents and carers a few days before you intend to make the display explaining the purpose of the display and asking if they could lend items which are used with water for a specific purpose.

● Ask a parent with a baby to come in and bath him or her for the children to watch.

Further display table ideas

● Display a collection of containers, some which hold water and some which do not, on a table-top next to the water tray. Sort the containers into appropriate sets.

● Cover a table with sheets of sand-coloured paper. Sprinkle on some dry sand and add some fishing nets. Display models of sea creatures and any shells that you may have in old collections. Include postcards and pictures of the seaside together with any toys that the children may have that are used to build sandcastles or other sand sculptures.

● Place cardboard boxes at intervals on a table and cover with blue fabric. Display a collection of shells in different shapes and sizes on and around the various levels. Label them with words that describe their different shapes, colours and sizes.

SCIENCE

Materials

A material world

Learning objective: to discover the variety of different materials around us.

What you need
A display board and table; newspaper, corrugated card and various papers; yellow and black plastic sheeting or bin liners; large piece of fabric; a collection of objects made from different materials such as wooden blocks and logs; cardboard boxes; plastic and metal household items; tin foil; Cellophane; household bricks and stones; a gun stapler; labels; reference books.

What to do
Cover the display board with newspaper. Drape the fabric at one side of the board and do the same with the plastic sheeting on the other side. Make a frame along the top and bottom from crumpled plastic bin liners. In the centre, fasten items made from different materials such as sheets of paper and card, plastic drinks bottles, Cellophane, aluminium cans and foil.

Cover the table with aluminium foil, newspaper and plastic sheeting. Arrange wooden blocks, bricks and boxes to add different levels, and intersperse with items made from plastic, metal, rock, paper, fabric and wood. Choose items that are interesting and unusual such as springs, metal icing-sugar sprinklers or coloured drinks bottles. Add suitable reference books and labels.

Talk about
● Where do the items in the display come from? Can the children find more things around the setting to add to the display?

● What are the items made from? Introduce the children to the language of materials such as plastic, paper, rock, wood, metal and fabric.

Home links
● In the week before you intend to start your series of displays, send a letter home to parents and carers. Explain the purpose of the series of displays and ask them to investigate materials at home with their child.
● Ask carers to play 'Spot the Material' at home and when they go out.
● Invite carers to contribute unusual, but not valuable, items for the display.

Young children come into contact with a huge range of materials every day. These inspiring display ideas will help them to learn about a variety of materials, their uses and properties

How does it feel?

Learning objective: to investigate and describe properties of different materials.

What you need
Display board with a clear area in front; brown and orange sugar paper; brown crêpe paper; different sizes of cardboard boxes; wood chips and shavings; sand; net curtains, nylon netting, orange and brown fabric; a variety of objects with different-textured surfaces such as fir cones, stones, pebbles, bark, logs, furry toys, wool and sandpaper; sheets of white card; black felt-tipped pen; PVA glue; stapler.

What to do
Gather the children together and invite them to investigate the different materials. Challenge them to shut their eyes and describe the texture of the different items using their sense of touch. Tell the children that you are going to put together a 'feely' display which will include lots of different textures for them to investigate.

Cover the display board with orange sugar paper. Drape the fabric across the top and down either side of the board. Add the net curtains and nylon netting to create a fuller background effect.

Create different levels in front with the cardboard boxes covered in brown and orange paper.

In groups, ask the children to use PVA glue to stick sand, wood chips or shavings to brown sugar paper to make texture pictures. As the children are working, extend their language of textures.

When the pictures are dry, attach them to the display board at an angle and a height where the children can touch and feel the textures. Make a border for the display by rippling brown crêpe paper strips around the edges. Arrange your collection of objects in front of the display board on the cardboard boxes. Invite the children to offer suggestions for appropriate labels for the different items. Write the labels on pieces of white card then double mount them on folded card so that they can be moved around.

Talk about
● What do we use to feel the textures of different objects? Talk about the importance of our sense of touch.
● Encourage the children to talk about the different textures. What else can they tell you? Do the materials feel slippery, dry, fluffy and so on?
● Which objects are hard? Which are smooth? Are there any objects which

Using the display
Personal, social and emotional development
● Develop skills of co-operation and turn-taking by playing 'materials dominoes'. Buy commercially made dominoes or make your own by sticking small circles of different materials to pieces of card. Before playing, ask the children to decide on the criteria for matching, such as the name of the material or a word to describe its texture. Play the game by touch alone – looking is not allowed!

Language and literacy
● Develop the language of texture using the display. Plan a daily activity to reinforce yesterday's descriptor before introducing a new one.

● Write a group poem to reflect the way the objects feel.

Mathematics
● Invite the children to choose two of the descriptors and to sort items from the display into sets according to these properties.

Knowledge and understanding of the world
● Plan a daily activity to sort the objects according to the texture criteria chosen by the children. This will support the acquisition of language detailed above.

● Take the children on a 'texture' walk around your setting. Choose one descriptor only to refine the children's understanding of that concept.

are both hard and smooth? Ask the same questions for the other textures.

● Look around your setting and identify different materials, then talk about the different textures.

Home links
● Ask parents and carers to help their child at home by finding groups of objects which are made from a material which is smooth, rough, hard, fluffy, slippery and so on. Encourage them to make this into a game at bath time, or when they are doing the washing-up.

● Invite one or two carers to come in to play the game in the setting with a group of children. They can also support the 'Materials' walk around the immediate area.

● Ask carers if they have any unusual but non-precious items which could form part of the display.

I can see through

Learning objective: to learn that you can see through some materials.

What you need
A large window at the children's height; Cellophane in various colours; a table; paint; card; cardboard yarn cones; PVA glue; spreaders; magnifying lenses; a collection of objects which can be seen through such as soft drinks bottles, biscuit dividers; plastic sheeting, spectacles, sun glasses, binoculars and telescopes; sticky tape; elastic; stapler; blue and red paper; sugar paper.

What to do
Invite the children to look out of the window. What is special about windows? Why do we need windows in our houses? Talk about other materials that we can see through and show some examples. Ask the children to help you make a 'see-through' display.

Position your display around a large window, divided into four sections with different-coloured Cellophane fixed in place with sticky tape. Fringe wide strips of Cellophane, and tape to the sides and top of the window, to make curtains and a pelmet. Add clear and coloured items made from see-through materials such as biscuit-tin dividers, plastic drinks bottles and so on. Put a table in front of the window and cover with Cellophane.

Ask a small group of children to make some glasses with coloured lenses. Cut out some spectacle templates from card. Cut out the two eyeholes if necessary, or let the children have a go themselves. Invite the children to

choose some coloured Cellophane to stick over the holes. Staple elastic to either end so that they can wear them to get a coloured view of the world.

NB: Remind the children that, even when they are wearing their tinted glasses, they must never look directly at the sun.

Make telescopes from cardboard yarn cones. Paint the cones and when dry, glue a square of Cellophane to the wider end. Arrange these on the table in front of the window display.

Cut the letters of the learning objective from blue and red paper and stick them to a large sheet of sugar paper, then tape this to the front of the table. Display your collection of transparent objects on and in front of the window. Include items such as spectacles, magnifying lenses, binoculars, telescope and the children's coloured spectacles and telescopes. Add labels for the different items.

Talk about
● Which part of our body do we use to see and to recognize different colours?
● Discuss the colours of the Cellophane. Help the children to understand that they can see through some materials even though they are coloured.
● What objects can you see through the window? What happens to the colours of the objects when they are viewed through clear Cellophane? What about coloured Cellophane?

Home links
● Before you set up the display invite parents to investigate transparent objects at home with their child. Provide a list of things that they are likely to find, such as water, glasses, drinks containers, video cases, light bulbs and so on.
● Talk to the parents about how this activity can be played as 'I Spy' and incorporated into bath-time, mealtimes, shopping and even watching television.

Using the display
Personal, social and emotional development
● Help the children to understand the challenges faced by blind people. Tell the children the story about 'Jesus and the Blind Man'.

Language and literacy
● Introduce language associated with transparency; see-through, clear, transparent, Cellophane, glass.

Mathematics
● Sort your collection of objects into clear and coloured transparencies, plastic and glass materials.

Knowledge and understanding of the world
● Cover a mesh bin with different coloured Cellophane. Place a different coloured object under the bin every day for the children to observe. What do they notice about the colour of the object when outside/inside the bin? Red objects placed under red Cellophane are particularly good for this. Develop the idea that the object has not changed colour, it merely looks a different colour.

Physical development
● Develop cutting and joining skills as the children make their coloured spectacles and telescopes.

Creative development
● Let the children create their own transparent pictures by attaching coloured Cellophane shapes onto clear Cellophane paper with sticky tape.

SCIENCE

Bright and shiny

Learning objective: to learn that shiny things reflect.

What you need
A display board and two tables; silver hologram paper; black sugar paper; foil sweet wrappers; foil paper in various colours; tinsel; black sugar paper; cardboard boxes; silver paint; twigs; shiny baubles; Plasticine; silver and gold coins; glitter; silver and gold stars; objects made from shiny materials including Christmas cards, fabrics, mirrors, saucepan, CDs, polished wood, tinsel, foil cake cases; plant pot; stapler.

What to do
Begin by showing the children a mirror. Let them investigate ways of holding the mirror to see both themselves and the room around them. What colour is the mirror? Tell them that they are looking at their reflection. Where else can they see their reflection? If necessary, suggest that water, glass and other shiny surfaces will produce a reflection. Invite them to help you make a display which shows how some materials reflect.

Cover your display board with silver hologram paper. Ask the children to glue shiny sweet wrappers other foil off-cuts to sheets of black sugar paper to make a border. Place the tables in front of the display board and cover them with a range of shiny and reflective fabrics and foils.

To make a tree decoration, paint a branch or twig with silver paint and sprinkle glitter over it before the paint dries. Decorate a plant pot by covering it with blue foil paper, tied in place with tinsel. Press the twig into a lump of Plasticine then secure it into the bottom of the pot. Hang reflective baubles and numbered gold and silver chocolate coins from the branches.

Make a shiny robot by covering cardboard boxes with foil. Stack the boxes together to form the body and staple on two arms. Use foil strips for hair and add a cone shape for a hat. Sit the robot in front of the display board.

SCIENCE

Invite the children to cover small boxes with foil in the same way, and stick these to black paper or card to create three-dimensional designs. These can be made into calendars for Christmas presents if you wish. Staple to the board above and around the robot.

Arrange the collection of shiny objects around the tabletops, interspersed with labels to describe the reflections and images created.

Hang CD and lantern mobiles in front and above the finished display and add labels of the children's suggested words to describe the display and the colours they can see.

If you create this display at Christmas time, there will be many more reflective materials to be found in the shops including cards, wrapping paper, tapes and present bags.

Talk about

● Talk about the colours that can be seen reflected in the displayed objects, particularly in the CD mobiles and hologram paper. The children should be able to see the range of colours of the spectrum. Relate this to the colours of the rainbow.

● Investigate the objects on display. What materials are they made from? Can the children find something that reflects an image made from metal, paper, fabric and plastic? Can they find something that is made from rock, stone or wood?

● Talk about the reflections that the children can see. Can they see their faces in the objects? Are they the correct way up? This will lead to a discussion about the shape of the objects and the effect on the reflections.

Home links

● Encourage parents and carers to talk about the images and colours reflected in shiny objects around the home and local area such as shop windows, highly-glossed paint, TV screen, polished wood and so on.

● Invite them to look for unusual items that reflect when they go shopping and if possible, ask them to purchase them and bring them for the display.

● Ask for contributions of threads and fabrics which have a 'shiny' content to add to the display.

Using the display
Language and literacy

● Introduce the language of colour and reflections and add the words as labels to the display.

Mathematics

● Invite the children to spot different shapes in the display. Introduce appropriate language to describe the shapes. Count the number of sides and corners.

● Number the silver and gold coins on the silver branch from 1–24 and use as an Advent calendar. Each day ask the children if they can find the next number on the branch. Make sure each child collects a chocolate coin at the end of the activity.

Knowledge and understanding of the world

● This display is particularly good for developing the knowledge and understanding of the colour spectrum. It is adequate for the children to know that the colours of the rainbow can be seen in the CDs and hologram paper at this stage.

● Use a paint program to make pictures on the computer using only the colours that the children can see reflected in the display.

Physical development

● Encourage the children to work independently to make their sculpture pictures. This will help to develop cutting and joining skills.

Creative development

● Use coloured foil to make pictures and patterns from circles, triangles, squares and rectangles. Allow the children to use their imagination.

THEMES ON DISPLAY
for early years

Magnet magic

Learning objective: to learn that some materials are attracted to a magnet.

What you need
A display board and table; magnets; small magnetic and non-magnetic materials, such as paper clips, nuts, bolts, plastic spoon, cork, cotton reels; iron filings in a secure plastic container; red and green backing paper; silver foil; cardboard boxes; information books, stapler, labels.

What to do
Cover the board and table-top with bright red backing paper. Add a border made from silver foil and divide the board with a diagonal line made from a strip of silver foil.

Place the magnets and a small selection of materials – both magnetic and non-magnetic – on a table. Gather the children together and invite them to spend some time investigating which objects are attracted to the magnets. Ask the children to draw conclusions about the different materials, then let them investigate other items around your setting. Once you are happy that the children have an understanding that magnets attract some materials and not others, explain that you would like their help to make a metal-eating creature which will only eat things that are attracted to a magnet.

Cover a cardboard box with silver foil and cut out a large slot for a mouth. Make sure there is enough space for the children to post items through the hole. Add silver foil eyes and hair.

Working with a small group of children, present them with a range of objects such as a rubber ball, a paper clip, a book, a key and a wooden bead. Give each child an item and a magnet and ask them if their item is attracted to their magnet. Allow all the children in the group an opportunity to check the child's decision. If the item is attracted to the magnet, invite the child to 'feed' the item to the creature.

When the children have successfully completed the activity, let them work with an adult to choose their own items to test. The adult can write down the names of those children who understand the concept.

Ask the children to draw pictures of items that are and are not attracted to a magnet and staple these to the display board, sorted according to the

Using the display
Language and literacy
● Introduce and consolidate appropriate language such as attract; magnetic; metal; not metal.

Mathematics
● Sort the materials into sets according to whether they are or are not attracted to a magnet.

Knowledge and understanding of the world
● Mix the objects up on the display.

Work with small groups of children putting the items back into the correct place according to whether they are or are not attracted to a magnet.

Creative development
● Put a small amount of iron filings into a transparent container and, for safety reasons, secure the container with a lid. Under close adult supervision, allow the children to move a magnet slowly beneath the container to create a pattern.

criteria onto each side of the silver strip. Add labels for the items and a sentence made from cut out letters saying whether the objects are attracted to a magnet or not. Replace your collection of objects on the tabletop for the children to sort into sets, together with books about magnets.

Talk about
● Discuss the materials that the various objects in the display are made from. Are all items made from the same material attracted to a magnet? Are plastic items attracted to a magnet for

example? Check your collection for items which could lead to misconceptions, such as metal paper clips with a plastic coating.
● Tell the children that it is important to keep the magnets away from any computers in your setting.

Home links
● Ask one or two carers to come into the setting to help with the sorting activity.
● Invite carers to contribute items to the display. Maybe someone has a strong magnet which you can borrow.

Materials

Paper twists and twirls

Learning objective: to learn that the shape of paper can be changed by twisting, curling and folding.

What you need
Fluorescent paper; yellow and black sugar paper; felt-tipped pens; strips of different-coloured shiny paper approximately 5 x 25 centimetres; pencils; scissors; stapler; sticky tape; glue sticks, cotton, gummed paper.

What to do
Tell the children that you are going to investigate different ways of folding, twisting and curling paper to change its shapes. Begin by stapling sheets of fluorescent paper to your display board in a patchwork pattern. Show the children how to make paper chains using red, blue, green and yellow strips of brightly-coloured shiny paper. Attach these around the edge of the board to make a border.

Give the children a sheet of yellow sugar paper each and invite them to use the felt-tipped pens to create handwriting patterns. When they have filled their sheets with patterns, demonstrate how to fold the paper into a concertina. Make these into fan shapes and staple them to the display board.

Provide circles of yellow sugar paper and ask the children to make colourful spiral patterns on them using felt-tipped pens. Cut from the outer edge into the centre in one cut to make a long spiral. Attach a length of cotton to each spiral and suspend from the ceiling above the display so that they catch the draught and swirl around.

Invite the children to make 3-D paper sculpture pictures to add to the display. Provide pencils and small strips of paper. Show the children how to wind the paper around the pencil very tightly so that it goes curly, and fold the paper into zigzags. Glue the shapes onto pieces of black sugar paper.

Add words to describe how curling and folding changed the shape of the paper.

Talk about
● Talk about how the paper changes shape when it is folded and curled.
● Watch the mobiles move in a draught of air. Describe the movement they make as they spin.

Home links
● Ask some carers to come into the setting to help the children make zigzag books, fold their patterns into fans and make the paper chains.
● Invite carers to make paper pictures and sculptures with their children at home. You may have some origami experts among your parents and carers who could show the children some of their sculptures.

Using the display

Language and literacy
● Invite the children to make zigzag books. Use them to record the children's stories.

Mathematics
● Investigate spirals made from squares, rectangles, triangles and circle shapes.
● Fold semicircles of paper into cone shapes to make hats. Decorate them with circles, triangles, squares and rectangles cut from gummed paper.

Knowledge and understanding of the world
● Make paper folds from different thicknesses of paper. Which is easiest to fold – thick or thin paper?
● Make spirals from different thicknesses of paper. Which spirals move the most when in a draught of air?

Physical development
● Copy the photocopiable sheet on page 77 onto yellow paper. Ask the children to trace over the patterns using felt-tipped pens. Fold along the dotted lines to make concertina shapes, then staple at the base to make fans.

Creative development
● Provide a variety of different types of paper. Invite the children to make them into as many shapes as they can by rolling, folding, curling and twisting, then stick them to fluorescent paper to make three-dimensional paper sculptures.
● Use paper fans as props in a dance of twists, twirls and curls.

Material textures

Learning objective: to discover that materials have different textures and that some have more than one texture.

What you need
A display surface; orange fabric; cardboard box; objects with different textures such as hessian, netting, felt, fir cones, bark, cotton wool, velvet, plastics; white and coloured card; computer with word-processing package; sorting rings.

What to do
This table-top display is an extension of the 'How does it feel?' idea on page 50. Cover a display surface with bright orange fabric and place a cardboard box on the surface to add height.

Arrange the objects on the table-top. Word-process labels for the materials and mount on coloured card, folded in half so that they stand up.

Place a sorting ring in front of the display. Invite the children to look at the range of materials and to choose one object. Talk about the texture. Is it hard, soft, cold? Does it tickle or prickle? Place the label and object in the sorting ring. Invite the children to investigate the display to find more objects which feel the same. Place another sorting ring in front of the display and choose an object with a different 'feeling'

descriptor. Repeat the activity, choosing different descriptors each time. Write the children's descriptors onto labels and add them to the display.

Talk about
● Talk about the materials that the sorted objects are made from. Can the children draw any conclusions? Are all the fabrics soft? Are all the plastics hard?
● Can you place any of the items into both sets? Which objects have several different textures?
● Encourage children to use the language of texture. Introduce as many descriptors as you can.

Home links
● Ask carers to repeat the activity at home to extend the children's concepts of textures.
● Send a letter home explaining the activity and inviting them to contribute items with interesting textures.

Further display table ideas
● Make a collection of plastic objects. Display these against a backcloth of plastic sheeting of various colours.
● Ask the children to bring in wooden items. Display on a wooden table alongside discarded natural wooden items such as pine cones, branches and logs. Use blocks of wood to create surfaces of different heights.

Minibeasts

It's a small world

Learning objective: to discover that lots of small creatures live in our world.

What you need
A display board; blue backing paper; cereal boxes; strips of green corrugated card; yellow, green and white paper; brown paint; a thick, hard-bristled paintbrush; PVA glue; stapler; sticky tape; pictures and models of minibeasts.

What to do
Cover the display board with blue backing paper and staple strips of green corrugated card cut in a scalloped pattern around the edge to make a border.

Cut lots of large petal shapes from the yellow paper and staple them to the display board in a circle, slightly overlapping, to make three sunflower heads. Make the centres of the flowers from three circles of white paper. Use a thick, hard-bristled brush to stipple these with brown paint and when dry, staple them in place in the centre of each flower head.

Glue or staple models and pictures of the minibeasts on and around the flowers. Cover the cereal boxes with green paper and place them in front of the display board. Add some potted plants or flowers and display a suitable poem about minibeasts.

Talk about
● Talk about the different creatures in the display. Help the children to name each type of minibeast.
● Read stories about minibeasts such as *The Very Hungry Caterpillar* and *The Bad-*

Tempered Ladybird both by Eric Carle (Puffin).
● Sing favourite songs and rhymes about minibeasts such as 'Incy Wincy Spider' and 'Ladybird, Ladybird'.

Home links
● Send a letter home to carers and parents telling them about your minibeast topic. Encourage them to identify minibeasts with their children both indoors and outside.
● Ask parents and carers to reinforce the message to children that we should take care of the small creatures in our world and the need not to touch them or disturb their habitats.

THEMES ON DISPLAY
for early years

Ladybirds, caterpillars and butterflies

Learning objective: to find out that insects have six legs.

What you need

Newspaper; white wax candles or crayons; leaf; leaf template; white card; scissors; paint in various colours; felt-tipped pens and crayons; black sugar paper; black pipe-cleaners; red and white paper; sequins; cotton; stapler; black and red letters; PVA glue; information books about insects.

What to do

Share the information books. Count the spots on the ladybirds. Do they all have the same number of spots? What do the children notice about the number of legs that the insects have? Tell them that all insects have six legs. Ask them to help you make a display which shows some of the insects around us.

If possible, mount this display around a doorway, as this provides the ideal shape for creating a hedgerow. Make branches and twigs from rolled-up sheets of newspaper and ask the children to paint them brown. Staple into position around the display space.

Let the children make large leaves. Show them how to press down hard with a wax crayon or candle to draw on veins, then paint over the veins with a thin green paint wash. Attach the leaves to the branches.

Give each child a ladybird outline cut from black sugar paper and ask them to paint it red. When dry, paint a thick black line down the centre. Let the children decide how many spots they would like to give their ladybird, then help them to cut the spots from black sugar paper and glue them on in symmetrical patterns. Staple the ladybirds among the leaves.

For the caterpillars, draw four circles, slightly overlapping, on white paper. Ask the children to paint three adjoining circles in green, and the last one in red.

SCIENCE

Add six legs, in pairs, underneath the green circles. On the red circles draw an eye with a black felt-tipped pen, and paint or draw on two antennae.

Ask the children to make bright blot-painted butterflies. Attach black pipe-cleaners for legs and antennae, and add sequins for eyes. Glue two butterflies back to back then attach cotton thread and hang them in front of the display.

Cut out two sets of letters to spell the learning objective – one from black paper and one from red paper. Staple the black set to the board first and mount the red set on top slightly to the right and above the black set to give a 3-D dropped shadow effect.

Talk about
● Discuss the way that caterpillars, butterflies and ladybirds move. They all move in a different way, for example caterpillars only crawl, ladybirds walk and fly, and butterflies only fly.
● Talk about what caterpillars and ladybirds eat. Caterpillars eat the leaves on the plant where the eggs are hatched. Ladybirds feed on small creatures that are also found on the plant.

Home links
● Invite parents and carers to help with the production of the ladybirds and butterflies. It is useful to have an additional adult to talk to the children about the pattern of the spots and the position of the legs.
● If possible, organize a visit to a butterfly farm and invite parents and carers to come along.

Using the display
Personal, social and emotional social development
● Help the children to understand the importance of caring for living things and their natural habitats.

Language and literacy
● Teach the children the nursery rhyme 'Ladybird, Ladybird'. Find other poems or rhymes to say about minibeasts.

Mathematics
● Make ladybirds with different numbers of spots. Talk about how the spots have to be the same on each side.
● Develop rhymes and games around the number six.
● Make a long caterpillar frieze out of numbered circles.
● Sort insect pictures, models and toys into sets according to whether they walk, crawl, fly and so on.

Knowledge and understanding of the world
● Talk about the life cycle of the butterfly. You could introduce this by singing 'I went to the cabbages one day' from *Tinder-box* (A & C Black).
● Talk about how insects move. Sing the song 'Caterpillars only crawl' from *Harlequin* (A & C Black)
● Use a simple CD-ROM or video to show the children the story of the life cycle of a butterfly.

Physical development
● Photocopy the sheet on page 78. Invite the children to trace over the dotted lines on the minibeasts' wings to develop pencil control and hand–eye co-ordination skills.

Creative development
● Allow the children to draw their own pictures of ladybirds, butterflies and caterpillars. Use these to make a border or add them to the main display.

THEMES ON DISPLAY
for early years

Spiders

Learning objective: to understand that spiders have eight legs.

What you need

A square-shaped display board; black backing paper; white paint; paintbrush; black tissue paper; black sugar paper; white and bright blue paper; sequins in a variety of colours; tin lids; silver spray paint (adult use); sticks; wool; black cotton thread; scissors; stapler; PVA glue; information and story books about spiders.

What to do

Begin by discussing spiders with the children. Tell them that although many people call them insects they are actually called 'arachnids', and are different to insects because they have eight legs, not six. Share the information and story books with the children. Count the legs of the spiders in the books. Look at pictures of webs and, if possible, show the children real webs around your setting or grounds. Invite the children to help you make a huge spider's web display.

Cover the display board with black paper. Using thick white paint, create a huge web in the centre so that it covers the whole board. When the paint has dried, use PVA glue to attach lots of sequins to the web to produce a sparkling effect. Cut out a giant spider's body and eight legs from black sugar paper. Add texture by gluing on scrunched-up black tissue paper. Attach the legs and add two big eyes cut from bright blue paper, then staple the spider in the centre of the web.

Invite the children to make little spiders in the same way as you made the large one, by adding scrunched-up black tissue and gluing on eight legs made from sugar paper strips. Attach thin black thread to some of the spiders and suspend them so that they hang at different heights and distances from the display. Staple the others onto the web.

On tin lids, help the children to carefully dribble PVA glue in the shape of a spider's web. This is less fiddly if you put the glue into a squeezy bottle first! Leave the webs to dry over the weekend, then carefully peel them away from the lids. An adult should

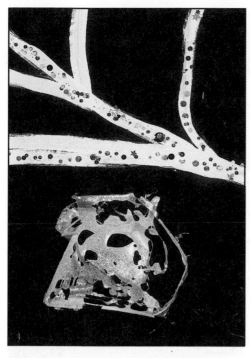

spray the webs with silver paint in a well-ventilated, open area, away from the children. When the spray paint has dried, staple the silver webs around the outside of the board.

Invite the children to 'spin' their own webs. Join two sticks at the centre in a cross shape and show the children how to wind wool around the sticks. Attach some to the display between the silver webs and suspend some from the celing so that they hang among the spider mobiles.

Cut the title 'Spiders' from white paper and staple to the display underneath the web.

Talk about
● Some children and adults may have a fear of spiders. Talk sensitively about the issues and help them to understand that although they might be afraid of spiders, they must never harm them.

Home links
● Ask parents and carers to come into the setting to help the children with the wool-winding activity.
● Ask parents and carers to make spider's web sewing cards using the photocopiable sheet on page 79. Ask them to glue the picture to thick card and make holes using a darning needle. They can then help the children to sew around the lines with coloured threads or wools.

Using the display
Language and literacy
● All children enjoy the rhymes 'Incy Wincy Spider' and 'Little Miss Muffet'. Develop the children's ability to listen for, hear and identify the rhymes aurally and orally.

Mathematics
● Talk about the shape of the spider's web. Reinforce the children's knowledge and understanding of spiral shapes. They will meet this concept again when making the 'Snails' display in this chapter and the 'Sealife' display in the Water chapter.
● Talk about the number eight. Can the children think of another animal which has eight legs? If you have already made the 'Sealife' display on page 46 then you could draw the children's attention to the octopus.

Knowledge and understanding of the world
● Go outside on a frosty or damp morning and look for spiders' webs. Talk about how they glisten with the frost and dew.
● Make spider biscuits. Cover a circular biscuit with black icing. Use coloured sweets for the eyes and liquorice sticks for the legs. Can the children think of other things that they could use for the eyes and legs? Remember to check for allergies.

Physical development
● Develop the children's pencil control by encouraging them to draw spiral web shapes on paper. Ask them to draw a spider in the centre of their web.

Creative development
● Create a spider's dance to the music 'piano scales' from *The Carnival of the Animals* by Saints-Saëns for the children to move around to.
● Invite the children to make shimmery spiders' webs by gluing strips of silver paper to black sugar paper.

Snails

Learning objective: to find out that some small creatures have no legs.

What you need

A display board and surface; fabric or backing paper in a neutral colour and a contrasting colour; gold and silver paint; pearlescent paint in a range of colours; white, grey and green paper; white A4 paper; felt-tipped pens; strips of fabric, ribbons and braids; egg shells; green, brown and grey paint; sponges; paint brushes; scissors; PVA glue; stapler; charcoal sticks; stones and leaves; Plasticine; computer; books and pictures of snails.

What to do

If possible, take the children outside on a wet day to look for snails. Ask questions about how the snails move. Can they walk? Why not? Back inside, discuss your findings. Tell the children that they are going to use lots of different materials and techniques to make some colourful snails for your display.

Cover the board in a neutral colour backing paper or fabric and drape the contrasting fabric across one side.

Give each child a snail outline cut from white paper. Ask them to paint the snail's head and body in gold or silver paint and its shell in two colours of their choice with pearlescent paint. Act as scribe as the children dictate a short story or description of their snail, and type these onto the computer. Print the stories and descriptions and attach them to the children's pictures before stapling to the board.

Encourage the children to ask questions such as 'What does a snail eat?'. Type these onto the computer, print them off and stick them to some of the snail pictures.

SCIENCE

Using the display

Personal, social and emotional development
● Talk about the need to care for the creatures that live in our environment and the importance of not destroying their natural habitat. Make a list of rules to display.

Language and literacy
● Develop the children's language by introducing new vocabulary including shell, foot and spiral.
● Make up a group poem to describe how the snails move, using plenty of alliteration. Use the activity to reinforce the children's phonic knowlege of initial sounds.

Mathematics
● Make a big display of spiral and circle patterns. Introduce appropriate language.

Knowledge and understanding of the world
● Encourage the children to use a painting program such as *TinyArt* (Topologika) to draw and practice spiral patterns. This will help to develop their mouse-control skills.

Physical development
● Invite the children to roll clay or play dough into long strips. Show them how to coil the strips to make snail shells, then add body shapes.

Use the photocopiable sheet on page 80 to make a snail stencil. Photocopy the sheet onto card and cut out the slots. Give the children sheets of white A4 paper and encourage them to sponge paint brown and grey paint through the holes in the stencil. When dry, cut them out and staple them to the display.

Invite the children to make other snail pictures using a variety of techniques. Paint some templates in browns and grey paint. When dry, use PVA glue to attach ribbons, braids and strips of fabric to the shell in a spiral shape.

Let some children apply a thick coat of PVA all over their shell shape, then sprinkle crushed egg shell liberally to the area. Leave the snails flat until they are totally dry and you will find most of the eggshell has stuck firm. Staple the pictures to the board among the painted snails.

Make smaller snails, using charcoal to add the spiral shape to the shell. Use these smaller pictures for a border for the display.

Finish the display with stones and leaves made from grey and green paper, stapled onto the board so that it looks like the snails are moving over them. Place some large stones in front of the display and invite the children to make Plasticine snail models to place on the stones. Add one or two books and pictures to the display.

Talk about
● Talk about snails' body parts. Draw the children's attention to the head, foot and shell. What other animals live in shells? Do they know other animals that have a foot but no legs?
● Talk about the different colours of shell that snails live in.
● Tell the children that it is alright to look at snails in their environment, but they should not pick them up or remove them. You could set up a snail garden in your setting so that the children can watch the movement and feeding habits of the snails. Talk about their natural habitat and how important it is that the snails are replaced where they were found.

Home links
● Send a letter to parents and carers a few weeks before you intend to make the display, asking them to collect and wash out egg shells.
● Invite some parents and carers to help the children make their snails and to write and print the stories and descriptions on the computer.
● Prepare a guidance sheet showing parents and carers how to do snail and spiral activities at home to help develop the children's pencil control and cutting skills.

THEMES ON DISPLAY
for early years

Worms

Learning objective: to discover that some small creatures live under the ground.

What you need
Pale brown backing paper; green tissue paper; sand and small stones; PVA glue; brown, yellow, black and grey paint; sponges; brown sugar paper; newspaper; natural-coloured tights or stockings; dried beans; chicken wire; strips of paper; stapler; information book about worms.

What to do
Share an information book about worms with the children. How do worms move around? Talk about where worms live and when we normally see them. Encourage the children to imagine what it must be like to live under the ground, then ask them to help you make an 'underground' display to show where worms live.

Spread PVA glue on sheets of pale brown sugar paper in patches, and stick on sand and small stones or gravel. When dry, ask small groups of children to sponge paint one third of the sheets brown, one third yellow and one third grey. When the sheets are dry, crumple them up slightly to give a textured appearance and staple them to the board in layers with the brown sheets at the top and the grey sheets at the bottom. Make grass from tissue paper spears and glue these near the top of the board.

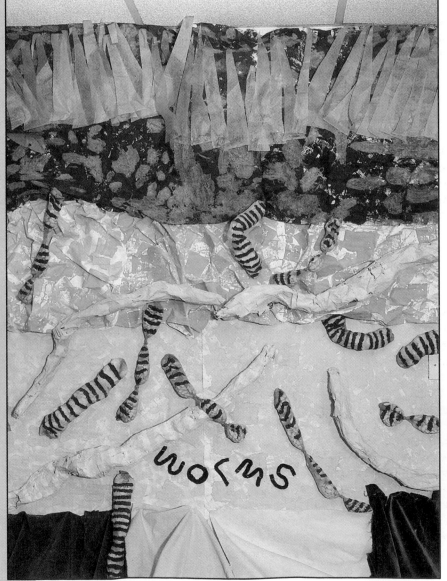

Shape lengths of chicken wire into worm shapes by bending at intervals. Under adult supervision, ask the children to cover the chicken wire by gluing on strips of white paper. When dry, let the children paint the worm sculptures brown, adding stripes if they wish. Staple the finished sculptures randomly onto the display.

Make some three-dimensional worms by stuffing natural-coloured tights and stockings with dried beans or small scrunched-up newspaper balls. Let the children add stripes using brown paint. Staple or glue the worms around and between the papier mâché worms.

Cut small worm-shaped letters from brown sugar paper to spell the word 'worms' and add these to the display for a title.

Talk about
● Which end of the worm is the head and which is the tail?
● Discuss other animals that live under the ground. Show the children pictures of rabbits, moles and badgers and talk about the different types of homes. What do we call a rabbit's home? What about a badger's home? How do we know that moles have been digging tunnels under the ground?

Home links
● Ask for support from parents and carers to help supervise the children as they make the chicken wire worm sculptures.

Using the display
Language and literacy
● Make worm shapes out of paper and ask the children to think of words to describe worms. Use a felt-tipped pen to write the words on the shapes.

Mathematics
● Develop the children's comparative language of length by comparing two of the worms from the display. Ask which worm is the longest and shortest? Can you find a worm which is longer or shorter than this one? Which worm is longer than your finger?

Knowledge and understanding of the world
● Tell the children about the importance of worms and how they help in the garden. Set up a small wormery. Fill a plastic sweet jar with different-coloured soils including sand, compost and garden soil. Add a few worms collected from the garden, then cover the jar with dark paper and leave for a few days. Remove the paper and show the children how the worms have begun to mix up the soils. Place small amounts of food on top of the soil and observe which foods the worms prefer.

Physical development
● In a PE lesson, develop the children's understanding of the way a worm moves. Consolidate previous learning about the way other small creatures move by incorporating this context into a planned progressive development of movement skills.
● Develop a photocopiable sheet of wiggly worms with dotted lines drawn along their bodies. Develop the children's pencil control and hand-eye co-ordination by encouraging them to use a pencil to follow the dotted lines.

Creative development
● Teach the song 'There's a worm at the bottom of my garden' from *This Little Puffin* compiled by Elizabeth Matterson (Puffin).

Ants, wasps and bees

Learning objective: to find out that some small creatures live together.

What you need

Green backing paper; brown fabric; cardboard boxes; yellow and black sugar paper; corrugated card; white tracing paper; hexagon templates (sides approx. 10cm); pencils; scissors; scraps of paper and fabric; tissue paper in various colours; brown paint; pipe-cleaners; felt-tipped pens; PVA glue; stapler; tub; flat brush; books with pictures of wasps, bees and ants; honey; beeswax polish.

What to do

Look at the books with the children. When do we usually see these creatures? What are their homes called? Tell the children that these creatures live in groups, and invite them to help you make a display to show this.

Cover the board with green backing paper and place the cardboard boxes in front. Staple one edge of the brown fabric along the bottom of the board and drape it over the boxes.

Tell the children that they are going to make a honeycomb from lots of hexagons. Demonstrate how to draw around the hexagon on yellow sugar paper and cut it out, then let them have a go. Invite the children to fit the shapes

SCIENCE

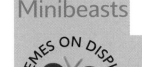
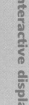

Using the display
Personal, social and emotional development
● Talk about the dangers of disturbing a wasps' or bees' nest. Remind the children to keep calm if a wasp or bee comes near them.

Language and literacy
● Talk about and name the homes that other animals live in.
● Read *Winnie the Pooh and The Honey Tree* by AA Milne (Mammoth).

Mathematics
● Talk about the hexagon shape, the number of sides and corners, the straight edges and the way they fit together without leaving spaces. What other shapes tessellate?

● Make a collection of items which have the number six in common.
● Count up to six every day.

Knowledge and understanding of the world
● Talk about other animals that live in groups such as birds, fish and people.
● Take the children outside to look for ants. Look around the base of trees and in leaf litter under hedges. Sugar can be used to successfully attract ants, but make sure you do not put it down too close to buildings!

Creative development
● Allow the children to make their own insects from collage materials.
● Let the children paint freely their own pictures of bees, wasps and ants.

together so that there are no gaps in between. Tell them that the shapes 'tessellate'. When you are sure that the children understand what you mean, glue the shapes on the display board to make a honeycomb.

Make flower heads by collaging petal shapes with tissue paper and fabric scraps. Cut a centre for each flower from yellow sugar paper and use a large, flat brush to stipple the surface with brown paint. Staple them to the display board. Make a few leaves to staple around the flower heads.

Add a tree trunk and branches made from strips of corrugated card. Ask the children to paint them using different shades of brown.

Let the children stick yellow tissue or fabric in stripes across templates of bees and wasps cut from black sugar paper. Attach tracing paper wings, and ask the children to draw on veins using a black felt-tipped pen. Add pipe-cleaner antennae. Staple the wasps around the flower heads and the bees on the honeycomb.

Ask the children to draw pictures of ants using red felt-tipped pens. Glue these around the base of the tree trunk.

Make extra bees and wasps to suspend above the display.

Display the books, honey and beeswax in front of the display.

Talk about
● Tell the children that ants, wasps and bees are insects, so they all have six legs.
● Explain that these insects have a sting but that they will only usually sting if they are disturbed.
● Talk about how bees make honey and beeswax.

Home links
● If you are lucky enough to have a parent or carer who keeps bees, invite them to come into the setting to show the children the clothing and equipment they use.

THEMES ON DISPLAY for early years

Creatures in the garden

Learning objective: to understand that lots of small creatures live in your garden.

What you need
Table-top; fabric with pictures of insects and small creatures or pale green fabric; cardboard boxes; large stones; small

pebbles; artificial grass or green fabric; mirror; plastic seed tray; grass or cress seed; soil or compost; flowers, pots; cuttings and small plants; lollipop sticks; small pond creatures.

What to do
Invite the children to help you make a miniature garden to display models of the minibeasts that they have learned about.

If you have fabric with pictures of insects on it, drape this over the table so that it hangs down in front and behind. If not, drape pale green fabric in the same way. Space the cardboard boxes along the table and cover them with artificial grass or green fabric. Place the large stones and small pebbles on the table to create areas of interest and intersperse with small pots with cuttings, flowers and small plants.

Fill the seed tray with compost or soil and plant grass or cress seed to create a lawn. Place the tray on the table. Make a pond by placing the mirror in a space and adding pebbles and small pond creatures. Finally, glue lollipop sticks together to make a fence and attach around the edge of the table.

Talk about
● Take the children on a minibeast safari. You can attract creatures in a number of ways including putting out logs and stones to attract woodlice and centipedes, sugar to attract ants and wet cardboard to attract various small creatures. Look around trees, hedges and flowers for ladybirds, wasps, butterflies and bees.
● Develop the sand tray into a garden. Include a log, stones and a range of small creature toys. Encourage the children to place the creatures in the appropriate place and question them as to why they put them where they did.

Home links
● Ask parents and carers to keep their eyes open for minibeast toys which can be used in the sand tray.

Further display table ideas
● Make a display of objects with pictures of small insects such as pencil cases, badges, cards, notebooks, erasers and so on.
● Display a set of wrapping papers and fabrics which have pictures of insects and other small creatures. Place realistic model minibeasts and magnifying lenses on the table for the children to observe the body parts of these small creatures.
● Display a collection of fiction and non-fiction books.
● Place a tape recorder on the table with a tape containing a collection of songs about minibeasts, such as 'Wiggly Woo' and 'Ladybird, Ladybird'.

Animal pairs

Match the animals who went into the ark together.

From wheat to bread

Colour in the pictures. Cut them out and put them in the correct order.

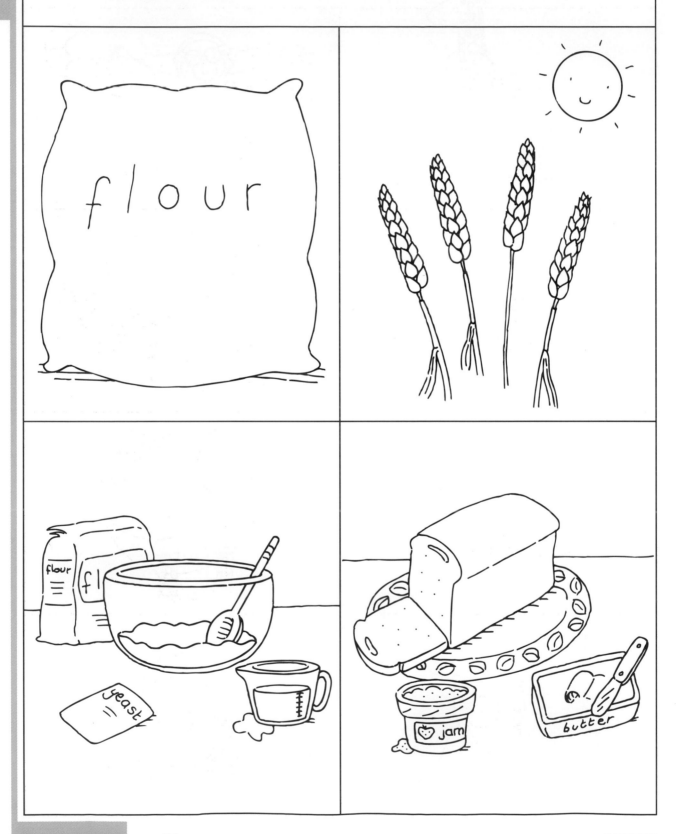

SCIENCE

Growing up

Colour in and cut out the pictures. Sort them into sets.

Colourful fish
Colour the fish.

Fancy fans
Trace and fold along the dotted line.

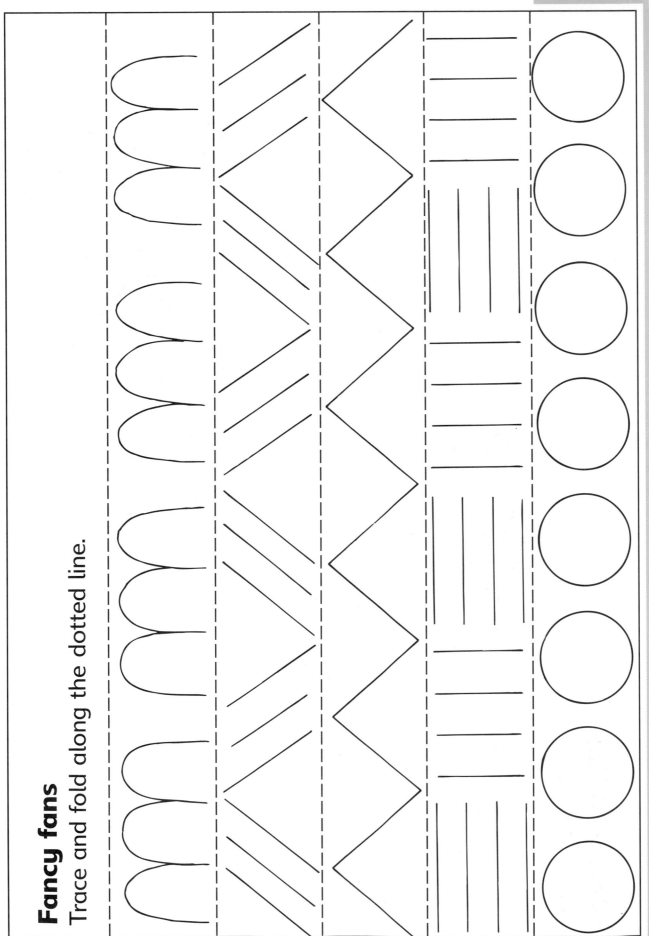

SCIENCE

77

Patterned wings

Trace over the dotted lines on the minibeasts' wings.
Colour in the pictures.

Spinning spider

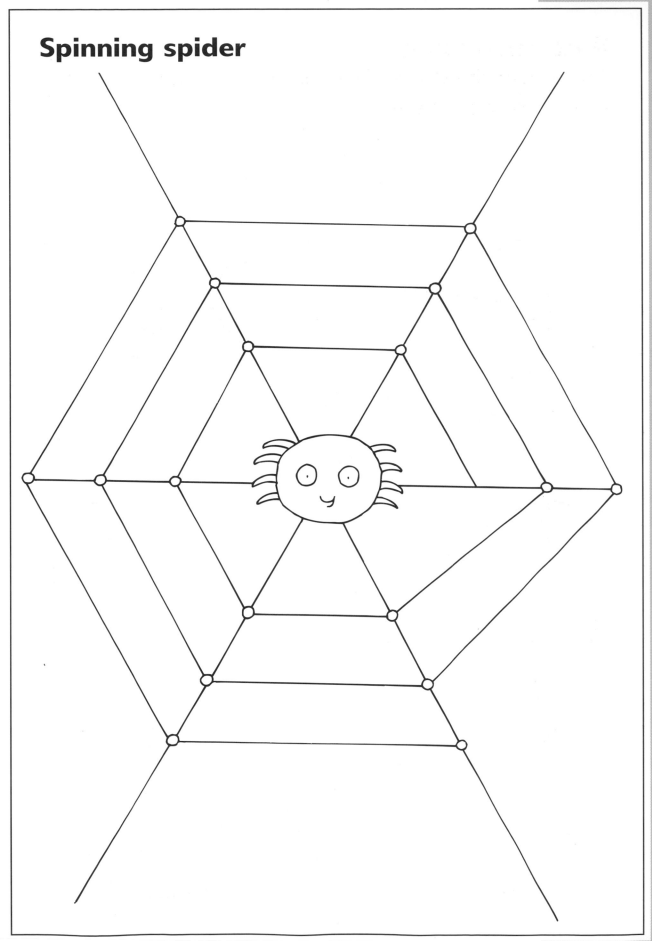

Snail stencil

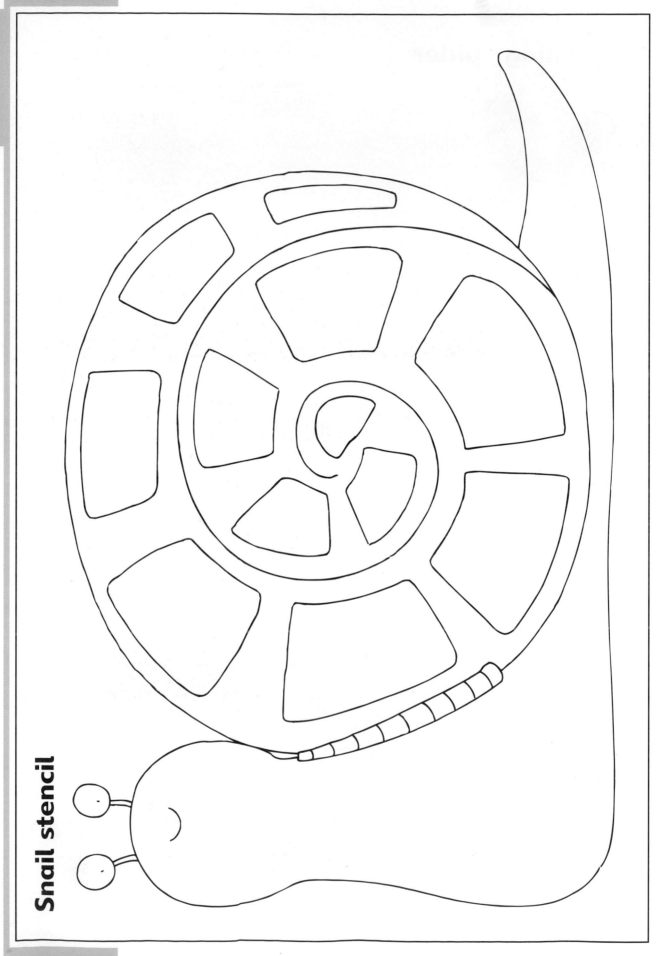

SCIENCE